Maggie's Christmas

Maggie's Christmas

Maggie Beer

Photography by Earl Carter

LANTERN

an imprint of
PENGUIN BOOKS

This book is dedicated to the memory of my Mum,
from whom I have inherited
a love of celebrations and ~ indeed ~ of life.

Contents

Introduction ~ 1

Crabbing at Port Parham ~ 9

Pre-Christmas Drinks ~ 51

Christmas Carols Buffet for the Choir ~ 87

Christmas Eve Supper ~ 129

Christmas Day Lunch ~ 161

Boxing Day Leftovers ~ 207

New Year's Eve Dinner ~ 241

New Year's Day Lunch ~ 277

Food for the Beach House ~ 303

Acknowledgements ~ 353

Index ~ 355

Introduction

From my earliest memories, Christmas has always been a real time of celebration for my family. When I was really little it was all about the presents (at the Sunday School Christmas picnics, somehow I was invariably the girl who was given the train set – or the equally unwelcome tea set!). Even so, going as far back as when I was five or six years old, the really special memories are of food. The first Christmas feast I clearly recall centred on the icebox on our back verandah working overtime in its attempt to keep the drinks cold, let alone all the food. From then on, Christmas meant a groaning table topped with the ham and goose plus chooks from our backyard. Gathered around the table would be our family, as well as friends without families of their own who were warmly welcomed. I don't know how Mum ever managed it as, whilst Dad would have orchestrated much of the logistics of the feast, Mum would have done all the work – as tended to happen in those days.

So it is that I've always loved this time of year. Those fond memories of a laden table are imprinted on my mind. Whilst I approach the Christmas season with much excitement, there is still a tinge of panic about how much needs to be done. Is it just that, at my age, Christmas seems to come around so quickly? Or is it a question of how I will juggle all the commitments of family, friends and the community, as well as the farming imperatives of crops that wait for no one? And, on top of it all, we'll try to pop down to Port Parham for some crabbing (see pages 11–45), if we manage to get away.

Nowadays, for us the buzz of Christmas starts in earnest in late November, when we hold our annual Christmas party for the staff of the Farmshop and Export Kitchen. Our Christmas gathering needs to be this early because the following three weeks are their busiest period all year, so we want to celebrate together in anticipation of the hectic time to come. The Farmshop team will be filling online orders and hampers, working against the clock until the last day Australia Post is able to deliver parcels in time for Christmas Day. At the same time, the Export Kitchen team will be working around the clock to fill Christmas orders that are two to three times the normal volume.

At this time, our neighbour starts to produce his Christmas speciality, the German yeasted cake, stollen. It's so moreish that we always have some on the lunch table at work, along with boxes of cherries, to keep everyone going. Honey biscuits are another Christmas tradition in the Barossa, with every bakery making their own, and someone at work always brings in their homemade ones to share, so much discussion ensues about whose biscuits are the best.

The next thing for Colin and me to juggle is attending the grandchildren's end-of-year concerts. We also start deftly putting out feelers to find the best gift for each of them – I find that their cousins generally hit the mark, more so than their parents, and definitely more so than we oldies. It's never about the value of the gift, but rather what is perfect for each child, in the hope that they will always remember it.

Our choir will have rehearsed a new batch of carols to perform one Sunday evening just before Christmas at a tiny church in a paddock outside Keyneton on the edge of the Barossa, where the locals gather for a variety of performances showcasing the colour and spirit of the community. Whether it's a semi-professional musical trio from Angaston, a youngster reciting or small groups and our choir singing, or the whole congregation singing together, traditions are alive and well, and there is such a feeling of goodwill. After the concert ends we all mill around, chatting and delighting in what a lovely evening it has been, with many staying on for a sausage sizzle. It's our tradition to head back home for our own sausages on the barbecue, and the night inevitably ends around the piano, with glasses of wine in hand. All these rituals add to the special atmosphere of Christmas in the Barossa.

I often say that, in coming to the Barossa, I truly live by the rhythm of the seasons, and Christmastime is no exception. Apricots are the first of the stone fruit to ripen in the Valley's orchards – and having recently acquired our own stone-fruit orchard, we are driven by the need to be ready for harvest. This means that hundreds of trays must be cleaned and about an acre of land covered in piping to hold the trays of apricots as they dry under the intense summer sun. Whilst an early season can mean apricots needing to be picked a week or two before Christmas, the onset of apricot season is usually heralded by Christmas Day itself. Therefore, it takes a great deal of planning to ensure that everyone involved in the picking and cutting can be with their family on Christmas Day and Boxing Day. At any rate, we are guaranteed of having at least some of our own fresh apricots ready to enjoy over the festive season. Then later, the (very South Australian) sight of a huge expanse of apricots drying is a promise of the treats in store.

Although we have thousands of apricot trees, we have only three Anzac peach trees, and their timing is generally spot-on. The maroon-flushed skin and juicy white flesh of these peaches is so fragile that they don't travel well, but luckily, Christmas is when they're ready. They are just perfect for Christmas and New Year's parties, especially when made into that iconic Champagne-based summer cocktail, the bellini. And how I love a party, whether giving or attending!

Despite the huge amount of organisation involved, the one aspect of the season that is never anything other than a true joy for me is thinking about the food for Christmas and its associated holidays. I have the advantage of tradition behind me so some things just fall into place, yet there is always leeway to try something new, as there are many more events to think of than just Christmas Day (see pages 163–203). Whether it's throwing a supper party for the choir (see pages 89–126), a drinks party for friends and colleagues (see pages 53–81), or factoring in all the advance cooking that needs to

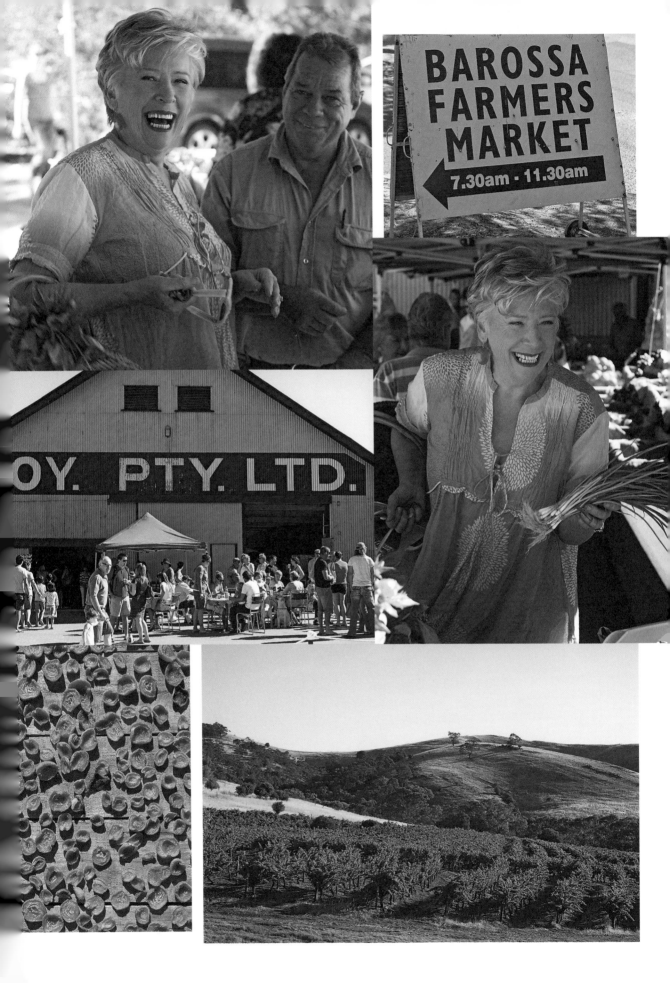

BAROSSA
FARMERS
MARKET
7.30am – 11.30am

OY. PTY. LTD.

be done before the New Year so Colin and I can take a few precious days' break after Christmas to tide us over until our beach-house holiday in January, it's never a chore.

I really mean it when I say I get excited about pulling the food together for all these special occasions, even though there are a few ingredients I must wait for Mother Nature to decide on for me. Take the first flush of figs, for example – will they be ready in time for Christmas? If not, who do I know growing figs in a warmer climate that might be able to help me out? Is there enough water in the dam for Colin to catch yabbies? If not, they are such a must-have on our Christmas menu (see page 167) that I've been known to order them in from Western Australia. When it comes to my grandchildren, I also need to make sure I have something special to offer my vegetarian granddaughter Zöe. And, do I take into account that five-year-old Ben will only eat the goose and not touch the salad or vegetables on the table, or leave that to his mum?

I must admit to a streak of extravagance when it comes to this time of year – and, if I am tempted by something special, I'll justify it by saying, 'but it's Christmas …'. This same impulse drives me to finish off all the things at home that have been on my 'to do' list all year. As I want everything to look beautiful, this is when the pomegranate hedge will be trimmed perfectly, the garden weeded and all sorts of things put away so that our place is as tidy as it will ever be – for Christmas!

On Christmas Day itself, the house will be overflowing with flowers, and even though the roses will be past their first flush, there will be vases crammed with every rose available, as well as the Christmas lilies that magically appear each year – I just love filling the house with flowers! The fridge will have had a complete clean-out, with every unnecessary jar removed to make space. The cellar will be raided for special wines, though they will have to be kept in the garage as the fridge will already be groaning with food. And in the aftermath of a full day's cooking, the chaos of my kitchen sink (captured by wonderful photographer Earl Carter on pages 204–5) will be enough to make every one of you feel super-organised because you would never let your sink get into such a state!

Even if Colin and I do manage to sneak away for a few quiet days after Christmas, we are always home in time for New Year's Eve (see pages 243–273) and New Year's Day (see pages 279–299). Then, if the season allows us, we are off to the beach straight away. Whilst I never want to live anywhere other than the Barossa, the sea is magical to me. It's the place where I can switch off, spending my time relaxing, reading, swimming and walking, as well as cooking with as much freshly caught seafood as I can get my hands on. When I feel the sea breeze, see the moonlight playing on the water and hear the hypnotic sound of the waves, I know just how lucky I am.

Crabbing at Port Parham

IT TOOK A WHILE FOR ME TO 'GET' THE APPEAL OF PORT Parham. As a Sydney girl originally, I hardly considered a tidal beach like this a beach at all, and I was shocked at having to search to find water deeper than my feet, unless of course I happened across a full tide. The Beer family shack has, without a doubt, the lumpiest bed, and the toy-box-sized bedroom hosts the occasional mouse plague, yet from my first trip there I realised I'd found something very special. I was truly taken aback by the great food discovery of freshly caught and cooked blue swimmer crabs, which Colin and his family had enjoyed during their trips to Port Parham ever since he was a young boy. I couldn't believe my luck when I first saw the copper of just-caught and cooked crabs being thrown over the old wire bed frame; left outdoors in the weather, it was well rusted and nobody cared. The cooked crabs were left to cool upside-down on this frame and I remember that, as soon as they were cool enough to touch, I got stuck into them! And that was a good 40 years ago now. When it comes to eating crab, the sweet flavour and wonderful texture of this crabmeat spoilt me forever.

Sometimes Colin and his brother Bruce still go out in the boat on the early tide so Colin can dive off the back, wearing a diving glove, and just scoop the crabs up. It is great exercise and our daughter Saskia loves to join in, but it's much too early in the day for me. There is also what we call 'walking crabbing', which is best done at dusk or night-time by lamp-light, dragging a baby bath around the waist. Whilst very tiring, the resulting good catch makes it all worthwhile.

However, the easiest (and our favourite) way of crabbing involves the whole family in the catch. We drive out on the jinker with Colin behind the wheel and the younger ones atop, all wearing old sneakers to save our feet from being bitten by the crabs. As soon as the jinker is deep enough in the water that the buckboard sits just above the waterline, we all jump in, armed with dab nets and a baby bath for the catch. There's lots of swooping of the nets accompanied by squeals of delight, not always yielding a result – there is a real skill to crabbing, but it's lots of fun trying.

There is nothing that compares to this whole experience. It's the excitement of the catch, followed by the unparalleled flavour and texture of the freshly caught and cooked crabs, which we eat on the spot with nothing more than fresh bread, salt, pepper, extra virgin olive oil and lemon. When the weather allows, we sit around at night by a bonfire and no one is ever worried about anything – this lack of stress makes it such a special place to us all.

WHITE GAZPACHO
WITH BLUE SWIMMER CRAB

Serves 6

We often hope for hot weather when we holiday by the beach, but, especially here in South Australia, it can be so hot that it is best to turn the stove on as little as possible. I've found that a chilled soup hits the mark all round and, given our climate, I wonder why they are not more popular. This Spanish-style soup fits the bill – the only downside is that you'll have to turn on the oven to roast the almonds before grinding them to really bring out their rich, nutty flavour. I tend to do jobs like this in the cool of the early morning or evening. Then all you need is stale bread, a good food processor and a last flourish of extra virgin olive oil before serving to make this easy, refreshing soup.

170 g flaked almonds
2 thick slices good-quality white
   bread, crusts removed and torn
   (to yield 70 g torn bread)
1¾ cups (430 ml) almond milk
1 clove garlic, peeled
sea salt
90 ml extra virgin olive oil,
   plus extra for drizzling
1 cup (250 ml) verjuice

200 g sultana grapes
ice cubes, as needed
finely grated zest of 1½ lemons
1 tablespoon lemon juice, or to taste
160 g picked cooked blue
   swimmer crabmeat
freshly ground black or white pepper
roughly chopped sultana grapes and
   chervil (optional), to serve

1 Preheat the oven to 180°C fan-forced (200°C conventional). Place the almonds on a baking tray and roast for 5 minutes or until light golden, checking them frequently to make sure they don't burn. Remove and set aside to cool.

2 Place the bread in a bowl and cover with the almond milk, then leave to soak for 3 minutes. Drain the bread, then squeeze out as much almond milk as possible and reserve to add later. Set the bread aside.

3 Crush the garlic with ½ teaspoon salt by dragging the back of a large knife over it on a chopping board a number of times.

4 Place the almonds in a food processor and process until finely ground. Add the soaked bread, garlic paste and 70 ml of the olive oil and process to blend. With the motor running, gradually pour in the verjuice and adjust the consistency of the soup by adding the reserved almond milk, a little at a time, until it reaches your desired texture; it should be quite thick. Adjust the seasoning with salt to taste, then transfer to a bowl, cover with plastic film and chill in the fridge.

5 Blend the grapes in the clean food processor until a coarse puree forms, then fold into the soup. Add 4 ice cubes to cool and thin the soup as they melt. Stir in the zest of 1 lemon, then stir in lemon juice to taste.

6 Place the crabmeat and remaining olive oil in a mixing bowl and season with salt and pepper. Mix together well.

7 Divide the soup among serving bowls, then place one-sixth of the crab mixture evenly in the centre of each bowl and sprinkle with the remaining lemon zest. Scatter the soup with extra grapes, then drizzle with a final flourish of olive oil and sprinkle with chervil leaves, if desired. Serve at once.

BLUE SWIMMER CRAB OMELETTE

Serves 2

My friend Marjorie Coats used to make the best crab omelette ever when she and her late husband Doug ran Seasons of the Valley cafe in Angaston many years ago. This omelette will forever be a part of Barossa food legend and is much missed, as is our great friend Doug. I didn't dare ask Marjorie for her recipe, so you'll have to be content with mine!

3 free-range eggs, plus 1 free-range egg yolk
sea salt and freshly ground white pepper
40 g unsalted butter
50 g picked cooked blue swimmer crabmeat,
   at room temperature

1 tablespoon creme fraiche,
   at room temperature
1 teaspoon verjuice

1 Place the eggs, egg yolk and a pinch of salt and pepper in a bowl and lightly mix with a fork. Heat a 20 cm omelette pan over medium heat and add 20 g of the butter. When the butter melts and sizzles, pour in the egg mixture and wait a moment for it to set, then shake the pan and tilt it down. Using a spatula, draw the cooked egg away from the edge of the pan to allow the raw egg to flow underneath and cook; the whole process should take about 1 minute.

2 While the omelette is still quite moist, add the crab and creme fraiche to one half, then flip the other half of the omelette over to cover the filling and turn it out onto a plate.

3 Add the remaining butter to the pan and cook over high heat for 2–3 minutes or until nut-brown. Remove from the heat and add the verjuice. Drizzle over the top of the omelette and serve at once.

Crabbing at Port Parham

Crab
Cakes

CRAB CAKES

Makes 8

What to do when you've caught more crabs then you can eat in one sitting? Use the leftovers to make crab cakes, of course! This is a base recipe so stick to the ratios I've given here, but you can do a lot of swapping of ingredients to make the most of what you have in the pantry. For instance, you can easily use whatever soft herbs you have on hand and, if you don't have any cream, use the same amount of mayonnaise, mascarpone or creme fraiche to bind the mixture instead.

2 tablespoons extra virgin olive oil, plus
    extra for shallow-frying
12 golden shallots, thinly sliced
100 ml creme fraiche
1½ cups (260 g) picked cooked blue
    swimmer crabmeat
4 tablespoons finely chopped chives
finely grated zest of 2 lemons
sea salt and freshly ground white pepper

CRUMB COATING
¼ cup (60 ml) milk
1 free-range egg, lightly beaten
½ cup (75 g) plain flour
1 cup (70 g) panko crumbs

1 Heat the olive oil in a frying pan over low–medium heat. Add the shallot and cook for 10 minutes or until soft and translucent, then remove from the heat and add the creme fraiche. Set aside to cool.

2 Combine the crabmeat, chives, lemon zest and creme fraiche mixture in a bowl and season to taste with a pinch each of salt and pepper, then mix until well combined. Divide into 8 equal portions, then shape into patties and place on a baking tray lined with baking paper. Cover with plastic film and refrigerate for 20 minutes to firm up before cooking.

3 For the crumb coating, combine the milk and egg for the egg wash. Dust the crab cakes in plain flour. Dip into the egg wash, then into the panko crumbs to coat evenly on all sides.

4 Preheat the oven to 140°C fan-forced (160°C conventional).

5 Heat olive oil for shallow-frying in a heavy-based non-stick frying pan over medium–high heat until hot. Cook 3 or 4 crab cakes at a time for 2 minutes on each side or until golden. Transfer to a clean baking tray. Keep warm in the oven while cooking the remaining crab cakes.

6 Serve warm.

CRAB AND AVOCADO SALAD

Serves 4

There are lots of wonderful food marriages for avocado, and many of them involve pairing it with seafood. I think of octopus and avocado (see page 330), prawns and avocado, and here I've used beautiful blue swimmer crabmeat with avocado – they just go together. As with all simple food, each of the ingredients must be perfect. I've already waxed lyrical about the blue swimmer crabs we catch and cook straight from the beach. You will also need to use a ripe avocado that hasn't been refrigerated. Unless you have your own avocado tree (and yes, I do, even in the Barossa) or a direct line to an avocado grower at a farmers' market, I suggest you buy unripe avocados and leave them at room temperature to ripen, timing their use so they never need refrigerating. When eaten like this, you'll fall in love with avocado as something special in its own right.

1 large or 2 small avocados
finely grated zest of 1 lemon,
   plus juice as needed
200 g picked cooked blue
   swimmer crabmeat
¼ cup (60 ml) extra virgin olive oil,
   plus extra for drizzling
sea salt and freshly ground black pepper
1 baby cos, leaves separated, washed
   and dried

2 heads white witlof, leaves separated,
   washed and dried
2 heads red witlof, leaves separated,
   washed and dried
large handful chervil leaves (optional)
Mustard Bread Rolls (see page 32) or other
   bread rolls, to serve (optional)

1 Cut the avocado into bite-sized chunks, then squeeze with lemon juice to prevent it from discolouring. Set aside.

2 Place the crabmeat in a large bowl, then drizzle with just a little olive oil to moisten. Add the lemon zest and season to taste with salt and pepper.

3 Mix the olive oil with 1½ tablespoons lemon juice or to taste. Season with salt and pepper.

4 Arrange the cos and witlof in a serving dish. Top with the crab mixture and avocado, then scatter with chervil (if using), season with a little pepper and drizzle with the vinaigrette. (Alternatively, place the cos, witlof and chervil [if using] in a bowl, then toss to mix and divide among 4 plates. Top each plate with one-quarter of the crab mixture and avocado, then drizzle with the vinaigrette.) Serve at once, with mustard bread rolls or your favourite rolls alongside, if desired.

Crab and
avocado
Salad

PASTA WITH CRAB
AND ROASTED SMOKED TOMATOES

Serves 2

The reason I chose shell pasta for this dish is that it's the perfect vehicle for capturing little mouthfuls of crab as you toss all the ingredients together. I'm tempted to say that it is only worth making this if you've caught the crabs yourself. However, after a recent stay with my friend Stephanie Alexander, when she presented some great frozen raw crabmeat from Shark Bay in Western Australia, I think you could happily use this instead. There is also the wonderful cooked and cryovaced spanner crabmeat from Noosa, which could be used if your beach is not a crabbing one.

140 g picked cooked blue swimmer crabmeat
½ cup (125 ml) extra virgin olive oil
finely grated zest of 2 lemons
¼ cup (60 ml) lemon juice,
   plus extra as needed
sea salt and freshly ground black pepper

1 quantity Roasted Smoked Tomatoes
   (see page 326)
200 g large shell pasta
1 large avocado
torn coriander, to serve

1 Place the crabmeat in a bowl, then add 2 tablespoons of the olive oil, the lemon zest and 1 teaspoon of the lemon juice. Season to taste with salt and pepper.

2 Peel the smoked tomatoes and discard the stems. Roughly chop the tomatoes to form a chunky pulp. Transfer the tomato pulp to a bowl, reserving the juices on the chopping board in a small bowl.

3 Mix another 2 tablespoons of the olive oil with the remaining lemon juice and add to the bowl of reserved tomato juices to create a dressing. Set aside.

4 Cut the avocado into bite-sized chunks, then squeeze with extra lemon juice to prevent it from discolouring.

5 Cook the pasta in a large saucepan of salted boiling water following packet directions until al dente. Drain and immediately moisten with the remaining olive oil (never rinse pasta under cold water to cool).

6 As soon as the pasta is ready, immediately toss the dressing through the hot pasta, then stir through the tomato pulp (the heat of the pasta will just warm it). Gently toss through the crab mixture, avocado and coriander, then season to taste and serve at once.

BLUE SWIMMER CRAB SANDWICHES WITH MUSTARD BREAD AND TOMATO AND SAFFRON JAM

Serves 6

This dish holds a lot of history for me as it dates back to the 'olden' days when Colin and I still had the Pheasant Farm Restaurant. I remember searching for a definitive dish to make the most of the catch of the day, after Colin and his brother Bruce had gone to the shack at Port Parham to stay overnight. They would go out on the early morning tide to catch blue swimmer crabs, which they would cook and pick with their mother, Flo. The crabmeat was so perfect that the idea of adding much more than a squeeze of lemon juice and drizzle of olive oil seemed unnecessary. To dress this up for the restaurant, I had the idea of making mayonnaise with the crab 'mustard' to stir through the crab, then using this to fill moist mustard-spiked bread. Of course, if you are at the beach and the idea of making your own bread is too much, then by all means use a lovely sourdough instead. I must admit one of my strongest food memories is of a crab sandwich Flo made for me in December 1969 on soft white bread (not the fairy-floss stuff you get today), so I wouldn't blame you one jot for making this sandwich a little simpler — just don't bail out on making the mayonnaise.

6 Mustard Bread Rolls (see page 32)
Crab-mustard Mayonnaise (see page 33),
   for spreading, plus extra to serve
480 g picked cooked blue swimmer
   crabmeat

peppery greens, such as rocket or cress,
   Tomato and Saffron Jam (see page 33)
   and lemon wedges (optional), to serve

1 Slice the mustard bread rolls in half, then generously spread the mayonnaise on the top half and add one-sixth of the crabmeat to the other. Serve with peppery greens, tomato and saffron jam, extra mayonnaise and lemon wedges alongside, if liked.

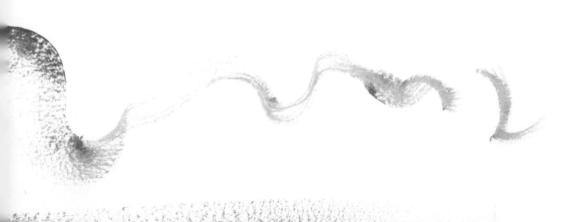

Crabbing at Port Parham

MUSTARD BREAD ROLLS

Makes 6

¼ cup (40 g) burghul
¼ cup (60 ml) tepid water
1 × 7 g sachet or 1½ teaspoons
   dried yeast
½ teaspoon caster sugar
1¼ cups (310 ml) warm water
¾ cup (210 g) wholegrain mustard

1 tablespoon maple syrup
2 tablespoons extra virgin olive oil,
   plus extra for brushing
3 cups (450 g) strong wholemeal plain flour
1 cup (150 g) unbleached strong plain flour,
   plus extra for dusting
sea salt

1 Soak the burghul in the ¼ cup (60 ml) tepid water for 20 minutes or until the water has been absorbed and the burghul has softened.

2 Meanwhile, combine the yeast, caster sugar and ¼ cup (60 ml) of the warm water in a small bowl. Dissolve the yeast by stirring it with a fork, then set aside for 5–10 minutes until frothy.

3 Mix the mustard, maple syrup, olive oil and remaining 1 cup (250 ml) warm water in a bowl.

4 Combine the flours and 3½ teaspoons salt in the bowl of an electric mixer fitted with a dough hook, then add the yeast mixture. With the mixer set on low speed, gradually add the mustard mixture and burghul to the bowl to make a soft, slightly sticky dough.

5 Turn the dough out onto a well-floured workbench and gently knead for 3–5 minutes to form a smooth dough (the dough might be soft and tacky so you may need to use an extra tablespoon or more of flour when kneading).

6 Brush the mixing bowl with a little more olive oil and return the dough. Roll the dough around the bowl to coat with the oil, then loosely cover it with a piece of plastic film. Leave in a draught-free spot for 90 minutes or until doubled in size.

7 Turn the dough out onto a floured workbench and knead gently for 2 minutes. Form the dough into 6 oval-shaped balls. Transfer the dough balls to a lightly floured baking tray and leave to rise, uncovered, in a draught-free spot for 30 minutes.

8 Meanwhile, preheat the oven to 220°C fan-forced (240°C conventional).

9 Bake the rolls for 30–35 minutes or until golden and they sound hollow when knocked on the base. Transfer to a wire rack and leave to cool completely before serving. (Leftover rolls can be individually wrapped in plastic film and stored in the freezer for up to 1 month.) (Alternatively, to make 2 small loaves, divide the dough in half and shape into loaf shapes. Bake for 45 minutes or until golden and they sound hollow when knocked on the base.)

CRAB-MUSTARD MAYONNAISE

Makes about 280 ml

Crab liver is yellowy-orange in colour, which no doubt is the reason it is known as the 'mustard'. In some parts of the world it is also known as the tomalley. It is found inside the shell and is sadly discarded, along with the shells, by most. It has a rich flavour and can simply be added to the meat of the crab, however you plan to eat it.

3 free-range egg yolks
¼ cup (60 g) crab mustard, if available
   (from 3 small crabs)
1 teaspoon lemon juice, plus extra as needed

½ cup (125 ml) extra virgin olive oil
½ cup (125 ml) grapeseed oil
sea salt and freshly ground white pepper

1 Blend the egg yolks, crab mustard and 1 teaspoon of the lemon juice in a food processor. You can continue in the food processor, but for the very best mayonnaise, transfer the egg mixture to a bowl and use a whisk. Start by whisking in the olive oil, drop by drop at first, and then in a slow but steady stream, followed by the grapeseed oil, whisking until the mixture is thick and glossy. Season the mayonnaise to taste with salt and pepper and add more lemon juice, if desired. Cover closely with plastic film and refrigerate until required. Use within 2 days of making.

TOMATO AND SAFFRON JAM

Makes about 1½ cups (375 ml)

pinch of saffron threads
1 tablespoon warm water
2 tablespoons extra virgin olive oil
½ onion, roughly chopped
½ cup (125 ml) verjuice

2 tablespoons red wine vinegar
1 × 400 g tin diced Italian tomato
1½ tablespoons caster sugar
sea salt

1 Place the saffron and warm water in a small bowl and set aside to steep.

2 Heat the olive oil in a small saucepan over medium heat. Add the onion and cook for 5 minutes or until softened and translucent. Add the verjuice, vinegar, tomato, caster sugar, ½ teaspoon salt and the saffron mixture. Bring to the boil, then reduce the heat to low and simmer for 30–40 minutes or until reduced and jammy. Leave to cool.

3 Store the jam in a sterilised jar in the refrigerator for up to 2 weeks.

WHITING SASHIMI WITH CAPERS, CHERVIL AND LIME

Serves 4

We all know that sashimi must be made using the freshest fish. And what better way is there to enjoy this than catching a whiting off the beach in the morning, then having sashimi that night? You can't get the same result from buying whiting fillets, no matter how good your fishmonger is. Whiting is best chilled whole, then filleted and sliced for sashimi whilst it is still really cold. Sashimi is my favourite way to serve all freshly caught fish – with the possible exception of oily fish – as well as lobster, squid, octopus, scallops and razor fish.

2 tablespoons extra virgin olive oil

2 tablespoons salted baby capers, rinsed and drained

1 × 400 g whiting fillet, skin-on, trimmed of bloodline, if desired, pin-boned

2 tablespoons chervil

2 limes, 1 thinly sliced and 1 squeezed

1 Heat 1 tablespoon of the olive oil in a small non-stick frying pan over high heat until hot. Add the capers and fry for 30 seconds or until just crisp and the flowers open. Remove from the pan and drain on paper towel.

2 Holding onto the skin, thinly slice the whiting with a sharp flexible knife. Overlap the slices on a serving dish or 4 plates. Discard the skin. Sprinkle the sashimi with the capers and chervil, then drizzle with the lime juice and remaining olive oil. Add the lime slices and serve at once.

Crabbing at Port Parham

Garfish with fennel and orange Salad

GARFISH WITH FENNEL
AND ORANGE SALAD

Serves 6

The Beer family shack at Port Parham gave me lots of firsts: waiting for the ocean water to come in with the tide; sleeping on a lumpy bed; absolutely no one stressed about anything; and the amazing sunsets that were as vibrant – or more so – than those of the Greek islands. Of course, this was also the first time I'd ever tried freshly caught and cooked blue swimmer crabs, as well as garfish. I'd never seen garfish before I went to South Australia. Once I discovered them, they became a firm favourite, especially when cooked simply like this, where you can almost eat the bones. The flesh is so sweet that all it needs is a squeeze of lemon juice.

⅓ cup (50 g) plain flour
⅓ cup (55 g) semolina
⅓ cup (50 g) cornflour
sea salt and freshly ground black pepper
6 × 175 g garfish, cleaned and scaled
extra virgin olive oil, for shallow-frying
lemon wedges, to serve

FENNEL AND ORANGE SALAD
2 bulbs baby fennel, trimmed with fronds
   reserved, very thinly sliced or shaved
1 tablespoon verjuice
zest of 1 orange, removed in long, thin strips
1 tablespoon lemon juice
¼ cup (60 ml) extra virgin olive oil
sea salt and freshly ground white pepper

1 To make the salad, place the fennel flesh and fronds, verjuice, orange zest, lemon juice and olive oil in a bowl and mix until well combined. Season to taste with salt and pepper. Set aside.

2 Mix the flour, semolina and cornflour in a shallow bowl and season with salt and pepper to taste.

3 Heat a 1.5 cm-deep layer of olive oil in a large heavy-based frying pan over high heat until it registers 180°C on a sugar/deep-fry thermometer (or until a cube of bread turns golden in 15 seconds). Meanwhile, coat the fish evenly in the flour mixture, shaking to dust off any excess. Place 2 garfish at a time in the pan and cook for 30 seconds on one side or until golden. Flip over and cook for another 30 seconds, then flip onto the side (backbone) and cook for 30 seconds or until just cooked through. Drain the garfish on paper towel.

4 Serve the garfish with the fennel and orange salad and lemon wedges alongside.

TOMMY RUFFS WITH CURRANT VINAIGRETTE

Serves 6

Now called 'southern herrings', these flavoursome oily fish will always be affectionately known as tommy ruffs to me, and are all the better if you are able to catch or buy really plump ones. The actual cooking time takes less than 5 minutes, so making this generates no real heat in the kitchen – as long as you cook the onions and fish in separate pans at the same time. This is so tasty it needs nothing more than some crusty bread to sop up the juices. Should there be any leftover, it is great refrigerated overnight as the flavours will really intensify.

130 g dried currants
50 ml verjuice
¼ cup (35 g) plain flour
sea salt and freshly ground black pepper
120 g unsalted butter, chopped
220 ml extra virgin olive oil
500 g tommy ruff (southern herring) fillets,
   skin-on (if unavailable, use Spanish
   mackerel or sardine fillets)

2 large red onions, finely chopped
finely grated zest of 3 lemons,
   plus ½ cup (125 ml) lemon juice
4 sprigs oregano
finely chopped flat-leaf parsley
   (optional), to serve

1 Place the currants in a small bowl and cover with the verjuice, then soak overnight (or microwave in a microwave-proof bowl on low for 5 minutes). Set aside.

2 Season the flour with salt and pepper.

3 Melt 60 g of the butter in a frying pan over high heat and cook for 2–3 minutes until nut-brown, adding 1 tablespoon of the olive oil when the butter starts to bubble to prevent it from burning.

4 Lightly dust the fish with the seasoned flour, shaking off the excess, then immediately add them to the pan and seal for 30 seconds only on each side. Transfer the fish to a deep serving dish large enough to contain them in a single layer, then set aside.

5 Quickly wipe the pan clean with paper towel, then heat the remaining butter over high heat until nut-brown. Add 1 tablespoon of the olive oil to prevent burning, then add the onion and cook for 3 minutes. Add the lemon zest and juice, oregano and currant mixture (this will change the colour of the onion from pale to deep-pink or burgundy). Remove the pan from the heat and add the remaining olive oil to balance the vinaigrette.

6 Pour the hot currant vinaigrette over the fish in the serving dish and leave to stand for at least 15 minutes; this will complete the 'cooking'. Sprinkle with parsley, if you like, then serve at room temperature.

Beer-battered mullaway with avocado

tomato
and red onion
salad

BEER-BATTERED MULLOWAY WITH AVOCADO, TOMATO AND RED ONION SALAD

Serves 6

My mother-in-law, Flo, taught me how to make beer batter for fish, which was appropriate given the family name! This dish brings back fond memories of family holidays catching fish at the beach, with Flo filleting them deftly, then having the beer batter on stand-by in the fridge (it's best when made the night before). I enjoy serving the fish with a delightfully fresh tomato, avocado and red onion salad; however, I only make this salad when the tomatoes and avocado are perfectly ripe.

1 × 1 kg mulloway fillet, trimmed and
   cut into 6 even pieces, pin-boned
extra virgin olive oil, for cooking
2 thick slices sourdough bread
lemon wedges, to serve

BEER BATTER
125 g self-raising flour
¼ cup (60 ml) light beer, plus
   1½ tablespoons extra, if desired
½ cup (125 ml) cold water

AVOCADO, TOMATO AND RED ONION SALAD
1 large ripe avocado
½ lemon
200 g baby roma (plum) tomatoes,
   cut in half lengthways
½ red onion, cut into quarters and
   thinly sliced
1 tablespoon extra virgin olive oil
sea salt and freshly ground black pepper
micro-mint or small mint leaves, to serve

1 Make the batter the night before. Whisk the flour, beer and water in a bowl until smooth. Cover and refrigerate overnight (if time is an issue, you can refrigerate for a minimum of 1 hour). Remove from the fridge and stir 20 minutes before using (for a lacier batter, whisk in another 1½ tablespoons beer at this stage).

2 To make the salad, cut the avocado into bite-sized chunks and immediately squeeze with a little lemon juice to prevent it from discolouring. Combine the tomato, onion, avocado, olive oil and salt and pepper to taste in a bowl and toss gently. Transfer to a serving bowl and sprinkle with mint just before serving.

3 Heat a 1.5 cm-deep layer of olive oil in a large frying pan over high heat until it registers 180°C on a sugar/deep-fry thermometer (or a cube of bread turns brown in 15 seconds). Working in batches of 2 fillets at a time, dip the fillets into the batter to evenly coat, allowing any excess to run off. Gently add the fish to the pan and cook for 1 minute on one side, then flip and cook for a further minute on the other side or until the batter is golden and crisp and the fish is cooked through. Remove the fish from the pan, then place it on the bread slices to drain.

4 Serve the fish at once, with the salad and lemon wedges alongside.

PAVLOVA WITH LADY FINGER BANANA AND PASSIONFRUIT TOPPING

Serves 6–8

When staying at the beach, you'll want to make mayonnaise for sure as it goes so well with seafood, so you'll definitely have leftover egg whites to use up. Pavlova was the first dessert I ever made (if you don't include an orange cake I baked for my grandmother when I was eight years old), whilst still in my teens, for what I would have grandly called a 'dinner party'. And today, I still love this topping, although my tastes have become more 'grown-up' as I often mix some creme fraiche into the whipped cream to add a little tang. I only make this when I find perfectly ripe lady finger bananas with black stripes on the skin. When the skin of these bananas is still only yellow, they will taste like eating straight tannin, unlike the more common Cavendish banana, which is ripe when the skins are just yellow.

4 free-range egg whites, at room
   temperature (from 59 g eggs)
240 g caster sugar
pinch of salt
1 tablespoon cornflour
1¼ teaspoons verjuice

BANANA AND PASSIONFRUIT TOPPING
150 ml thickened cream
150 ml creme fraiche
3–4 ripe lady finger bananas
2 teaspoons verjuice
⅓ cup (80 ml) passionfruit pulp
   (from 4 large passionfruit)

1 Preheat the oven to 140°C fan-forced (160°C conventional). Line a baking tray with baking paper and use a pencil to draw a 20 cm round on the paper, then turn the paper over.

2 Place the egg whites in the bowl of an electric mixer, making sure the bowl and whisk are clean and dry. Whisk until very soft peaks form, then, with the motor running, slowly add the caster sugar and salt. Continue to whisk until all the sugar has dissolved (rub a small amount of meringue between your fingers – if it feels slightly grainy continue to whisk). Fold through the cornflour and verjuice. Spoon the meringue onto the marked 20 cm round, mounding it as you go.

3 Place the meringue in the oven and immediately reduce the oven temperature to 120°C fan-forced (140°C conventional). Bake the meringue for 1 hour 20 minutes. Turn off the oven and leave the meringue inside with the oven door slightly ajar (use a wooden spoon to wedge the door open) to cool for 30 minutes.

4 Just before serving, prepare the topping. Place the cream in the clean and dry bowl of the electric mixer and whisk until soft peaks form. Fold in the creme fraiche. Slice the bananas, then immediately place in a bowl and pour over the verjuice to coat to prevent it from discolouring.

5 Spread the whipped cream mixture over the cooled meringue and top with the banana. Drizzle the passionfruit pulp over and serve.

Pavlova with lady finger
banana and

passion fruit topping

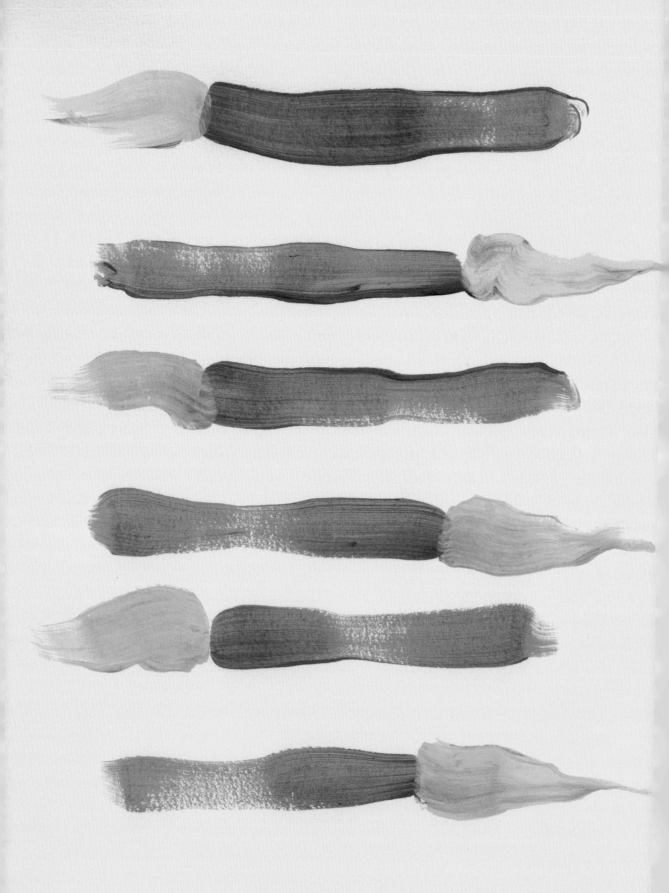

Pre-Christmas Drinks

I DO LOVE A GOOD PARTY, WHICH FOR ME MEANS PUTTING on beautiful food without getting into a terrible bind about it. In fact, it's a matter of pride that I've brought together a selection of dishes here that is within everyone's bounds, so you can pull this off as well without getting too stressed about it – and enjoy the party as much as your guests! I certainly don't consider it cheating to buy in a dish if you need to, as long as the quality is there. I would absolutely take up any offers of help from anyone who loves to cook, as long as they're not offended when you designate a specific dish so that the whole menu fits together. I also try very hard to do as much work as I can in advance, and to make sure I have some vegetarian and gluten-free dishes so no one misses out. And I often bribe a grandchild to help on the night.

Whilst any sort of party takes planning, I have different ways of thinking about this depending on the occasion. Sometimes it's easiest to follow a theme, for instance going Middle Eastern, Italian or French, whether you're planning to just have a few people over for drinks or it's the whole shebang. For a drinks do, I try to offer as much finger food as I can, whilst aiming to provide as much substance as possible, in case all the 'excitement' gets the better of one of the guests.

You need to plan to bring out the food in waves, so it makes sense to start with cold offerings that you've made in advance. It's a good idea to minimise any cooking once the guests have arrived, taking into account the limits of your kitchen equipment. The times I've come unstuck happened when I underestimated how long the last-minute deep-frying would take. My advice is to wait till you've cooked the beautiful zucchini flowers I've included here before you join in the revelry, and let the easier hot food follow; that is, the dishes coming straight from the oven.

The other bonus of finger food is that it minimises the need to borrow or hire extra cutlery and crockery for the night – although glasses are usually another matter. I must admit I have quite a coterie of extra kitchen implements in my cupboards. I adore old things and have collected lots of plates from bric-a-brac shops over the years. I love placing a stack of plates on the table, mismatched yet of the same era so that they just go together. I've also built up a supply of shot glasses, plus tiny ceramic dishes of all the same size, which I bought for a song from the community op-shop – all of these come to the fore at a party.

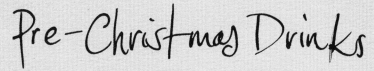

Pre-Christmas Drinks

Menu for 8

Cucumber and verjuice jelly with oysters ~ 58

Bocconcini balls with dukkah ~ 59

Persian feta-stuffed zucchini flowers ~ 64

Soft-boiled eggs on toast with caper, raisin and basil salsa ~ 67

Olive-oil, olive and orange brioche ~ 70

Chicken schnitters ~ 73

Chicken, prune and lemon tarts with pine-nut mayonnaise ~ 74

Lamb kibbeh ~ 76

Lemon-glazed chicken wings ~ 80

Chestnut and chocolate pots with pineapple ~ 81

Cucumber and verjuice jelly with oysters

CUCUMBER AND VERJUICE JELLY WITH OYSTERS

Serves 10 as part of a buffet

It always seems ironic that we most often think of using oysters for summer celebrations, particularly Christmas, yet this is the time when many oysters are spawning and not at their best. There are some from cooler climates such as in Tasmania, but for local oysters the Turner family from Cleve in South Australia (among others in the area) are now propagating an oyster that doesn't spawn, called triploid oysters, so they can supply a reliable source of high-quality oysters year-round. And I have to admit that, whenever I get the chance, I search out the native Angasi oysters. Freshly shucked oysters served on a bed of ice is about as good as it gets, so an oyster knife is a useful addition to your kitchen tool drawer. Along with owning one of these comes the confidence to use it, and that comes from two 'p's': practice and protection. I suggest you drape a clean tea towel around the hand that holds the oysters until you've developed your shucking skills. Setting cucumber in verjuice jelly is so refreshing; it's the perfect accompaniment for beautiful oysters. It's just about getting the set of the jelly right so it wobbles a little as you serve it.

¾ cup (180 ml) verjuice
1 tablespoon chopped dill
4 × 2 g gold-strength gelatine leaves
2 cups (500 ml) cold water
1 telegraph (continental) cucumber (about 400 g), peeled, cut in half lengthways, seeded and roughly chopped (to yield 250 g)

1 teaspoon caster sugar
sea salt
30 oysters, freshly shucked
extra virgin olive oil, for drizzling

1 Place the verjuice in a small stainless-steel saucepan over low–medium heat, then bring just to a simmer, being careful not to let it boil or the verjuice will become cloudy. Remove from the heat, add the dill, then set aside to infuse for 10 minutes.

2 Soak the gelatine leaves in a bowl with the cold water for 5 minutes or until softened. Remove the gelatine and squeeze out any excess liquid. Add to the warm verjuice and stir until the gelatine has dissolved. Set aside to cool.

3 Place the cucumber, caster sugar and ½ teaspoon salt in a blender and blend until a puree forms. Transfer to a mixing bowl and set aside.

4 Strain the cooled verjuice mixture into the cucumber puree and stir to combine well (there should be 400 ml and no less than 1½ cups [375 ml]). Line an 18 cm × 13 cm plastic container or baking dish with plastic film, then pour in the verjuice and cucumber mixture to form a 1 cm-thick layer. Refrigerate the jelly for 6 hours or until set.

5 Carefully turn the jelly out onto a chopping board, then cut into 1 cm dice.

6 Place the oysters on a platter or divide among small plates, then top each oyster with a cube of jelly. Drizzle the tiniest amount of olive oil over and serve.

BOCCONCINI BALLS WITH DUKKAH

Serves 10 as part of a buffet

The first time I tried this idea I deep-fried these little morsels in extra virgin olive oil. Whilst the result tasted fantastic, it was tricky to time the cooking perfectly so that they were warm but not melted inside, and the crust stayed on rather than falling off into the oil and burning. The solution was to bake them in the oven and cool them a little before serving. The secret of success is to be sure of the quality of your bocconcini, so find one you like before making this as some brands have the texture of little bullets when raw. As delightful as these are, if you're running short of time and your guests have arrived, just lay out the drained bocconcini balls with a dish each of extra virgin olive oil and dukkah for dipping. This way, rather than handing these around, your guests can help themselves.

2 × 220 g tubs fresh bocconcini (14 bocconcini balls)

2 tablespoons extra virgin olive oil, plus extra for drizzling

100 g dukkah (available from specialty food stores)

14 small caperberries, cut in half

1 Preheat the oven to 200°C fan-forced (220°C conventional).

2 Drain the brine from the bocconcini, then place the bocconcini on a plate and drizzle with extra olive oil. Place the dukkah in a shallow bowl or plate, then roll the bocconcini in the dukkah, gently pressing to coat evenly.

3 Transfer the bocconcini to a baking tray lined with baking paper. Heat the bocconcini in the oven for 5–6 minutes, then remove just before they melt.

4 Leave the bocconcini to cool for just a minute so as not to burn your mouth. Toss the caperberries in the olive oil, then place on a serving platter with the warm bocconcini. Serve at once.

Bocconcini balls
with
dukkah

Persian
feta-stuffed
zucchini flowers

PERSIAN FETA-STUFFED ZUCCHINI FLOWERS

Makes 10

The best zucchini flowers to cook are the ones I've grown myself as I can choose the male flowers (those attached to a stem, not to a small zucchini). Their larger, more open flowers have the dual advantage of a bigger area to stuff and less risk of tearing the fragile petals. However, even if I've planted my zucchini crop early enough that they're flowering in December, I can't count on having enough flowers to cater for a party so I order them from my greengrocer. Bought zucchini flowers usually come with the baby zucchini attached, so I've written this recipe for these. If one of my grandchildren helped me with this fiddly job, I'd be better off with the aid of their delicate fingers rather than my well-worked ones – that is, if I bothered to take the stamens out of the bought flowers, which have the added complication of being so much harder to handle due to having been refrigerated.

10 zucchini (courgette) flowers
100 g Persian feta, cut into 10 even pieces
10 anchovy fillets
2 cups (500 ml) extra virgin olive oil
plain flour, for dusting
lemon wedges, to serve

SEMOLINA BATTER
¼ cup (35 g) plain flour
¼ cup (35 g) cornflour
¼ cup (40 g) semolina
pinch of baking powder
½ cup (125 ml) milk

1 To make the batter, sift the flours, semolina and baking powder into a bowl, then whisk in the milk until smooth. Set aside (the batter will thicken while you prepare the zucchini flowers).

2 Carefully open each zucchini flower and place a piece of feta and an anchovy fillet inside, then gently twist the top of the flower shut to enclose the filling (there is no need to remove the stamens).

3 Heat the olive oil in a deep frying pan (mine is 30 cm deep) until it registers 180°C on a sugar/deep-fry thermometer (or a cube of bread sizzles in 15 seconds when added to the pan). Working with 1 zucchini flower at a time, dip it first into the flour and then into the batter, allowing any excess batter to drain, then carefully place it in the hot oil. Fry for 1 minute, then flip and fry for another 30 seconds or until golden brown.

4 Remove from the pan and drain on paper towel. Serve hot with lemon wedges alongside and eat immediately.

SOFT-BOILED EGGS ON TOAST WITH CAPER, RAISIN AND BASIL SALSA

Serves 10 as part of a buffet

Soft-boiled eggs are a great favourite with my family. Our chooks eat the most amazing amount of green feed so the egg yolks are so golden they almost look fake – I can assure you they are not. If you don't have your own chooks, go to the trouble of getting the best eggs you can buy. The salsa is great made in advance so the flavours develop, but I like to boil the eggs just before my guests arrive so I don't need to refrigerate them before serving.

10 free-range eggs, at room temperature
sea salt
ice cubes
1 sourdough baguette, cut into
   20 × 1 cm-thick slices

CAPER, RAISIN AND BASIL SALSA
¼ cup (40 g) seedless raisins
2 tablespoons verjuice
¼ cup (50 g) salted baby capers,
   rinsed and drained
1 tablespoon lemon zest, removed in long,
   thin strips
3 tablespoons basil, very thinly sliced
1 tablespoon extra virgin olive oil,
   plus extra for drizzling
2 teaspoons vino cotto

1 To make the salsa, place the raisins and verjuice in a small microwave-safe bowl, then cover with plastic film and microwave on the low setting for 5 minutes. Leave to stand for 5 minutes, then drain and discard any verjuice not absorbed. Place the soaked raisins and capers on a chopping board and roughly chop. Transfer to a small bowl, then stir in the lemon zest, basil, olive oil and vino cotto and set aside until required. (Makes about ⅔ cup [160 ml].)

2 Place the eggs in a saucepan of cold water with 2 teaspoons salt to inhibit leaking if their shells crack. Bring to the boil, then cook for 4 minutes exactly. Carefully transfer the eggs to a bowl of iced water, then leave for 1 minute to prevent them cooking any further. Remove and peel while still warm, then leave to cool completely.

3 Preheat the oven griller to medium–high heat. Place the bread slices on a baking tray and grill for 2 minutes or until golden, then flip and grill for another 1 minute or until golden.

4 Cut the cooled eggs in half with a sharp knife dipped in hot water. Place an egg half on each slice of bread, then spoon a teaspoon of salsa on top. Drizzle with olive oil, then serve.

Olive-oil, olive and orange brioche

OLIVE-OIL, OLIVE AND ORANGE BRIOCHE

Serves 10

Having often made brioche with olive oil, I came up with the idea of adding lots of orange zest and our home-grown olives after stopping by a Greek bakery in Adelaide and tasting a brioche roulade filled with olives. I thought it such a brilliant idea for a party, but once you've tried this, you won't need the excuse of entertaining to want to make it again and again. Try the brioche warm with unsalted butter, or serve it with fresh curd or any soft ripe cheese alongside. Leftovers make the most moreish toast imaginable, with lots of butter too, of course!

1 × 7 g sachet or 1½ teaspoons dried yeast
1½ teaspoons caster sugar
1 cup (250 ml) lukewarm water
¼ cup (60 ml) extra virgin olive oil
3 × 55 g free-range eggs
finely grated zest of 3 oranges
4½ cups (675 g) unbleached strong plain
   flour, plus extra for dusting
sea salt
1 tablespoon milk, beaten with
   1 free-range egg yolk
unsalted butter, to serve (optional)

OLIVE AND ORANGE FILLING
400 g kalamata olives, pitted (to yield
   300 g) and thickly sliced
1–2 tablespoons finely grated orange zest
2 tablespoons finely grated lemon zest
4 tablespoons freshly picked oregano leaves
1 tablespoon extra virgin olive oil

1 Mix the yeast, caster sugar and lukewarm water in the bowl of an electric mixer fitted with a dough hook. Set aside for 10 minutes or until frothy. Add the olive oil, eggs and orange zest and stir to combine.

2 Mix the flour and 3 teaspoons salt in a bowl, then, with the mixer on low speed, add the flour to the yeast mixture, a little at a time, until the dough just comes together to form a ball. Turn the dough out onto a lightly floured workbench and knead for 10 minutes or until soft and satiny, adding a little extra flour if it becomes too sticky. Return the dough to the bowl and cover tightly with plastic film, then leave to prove in a warm spot for 4 hours or until doubled in size.

3 To prepare the filling, mix the olives, orange and lemon zest, oregano and olive oil. Set aside.

4 Turn the dough out onto a lightly floured workbench and knead for 8 minutes; don't knock it back. (Doughs with a higher fat content such as this one struggle to rise again if knocked back.) Cover the bowl loosely with plastic film and leave the dough to rest for 45 minutes–1 hour until it does not spring back when pushed with a finger and can easily be rolled out.

5 Meanwhile, preheat the oven to 220°C fan-forced (240°C conventional).

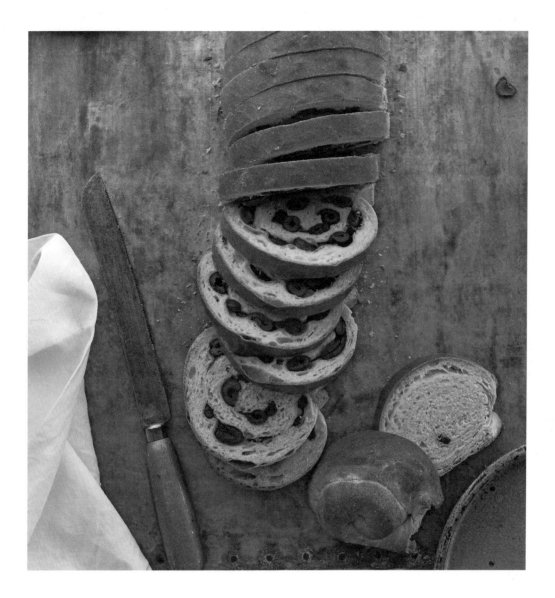

6 Roll and shape the dough into a 38 cm × 20 cm rectangle. Brush the egg yolk mixture over the surface of the dough. Spread the olive and orange filling over, leaving a 4 mm border along one long end. Roll the dough tightly to seal in the filling like a roulade, then brush the edge with the egg yolk mixture to seal. Place on a lightly floured baking tray with the seam-side down. Brush the egg yolk mixture over the dough.

7 Bake the brioche for 10 minutes, then reduce the oven temperature to 180°C fan-forced (200°C conventional) and bake for a further 30 minutes or until golden. Transfer the brioche to a wire rack and leave to cool.

8 Cut into slices to serve. This is wonderful enjoyed warm, and totally indulgent when served with a slathering of unsalted butter.

CHICKEN SCHNITTERS

Serves 10 as part of a buffet

It's always a good idea to offer something more substantial when you're having a drinks party for friends, even if you're not really supplying dinner. From an organisational point of view, it's even better when you can have everything made beforehand, and these warm sandwiches fit the bill. The filling can even be made the day before and refrigerated, and the first grill of the bread completed before your guests arrive, then placed on baking trays, ready for you to assemble and heat 15 minutes before you wish to serve them.

600 g free-range chicken thigh fillets, skin-on, cut into 2 cm pieces
sea salt
90 g unsalted butter, chopped
1½ tablespoons extra virgin olive oil, plus extra for brushing
2 small bulbs fennel, cores removed and discarded and remainder thinly sliced
2 tablespoons verjuice
⅓ cup (80 ml) chicken stock

1 preserved lemon quarter, flesh removed and discarded, rind rinsed and finely chopped
50 g kalamata olives, pitted and roughly chopped
5 × 18 cm wholemeal pita breads
handful flat-leaf parsley, roughly chopped
150 g Persian feta, cut into 1 cm dice
freshly ground black pepper

1   Sprinkle the chicken with 2 teaspoons salt. Heat a large heavy-based non-stick frying pan over medium–high heat. Melt 30 g of the butter and cook for 2–3 minutes until nut-brown, adding 2 teaspoons of the olive oil when the butter starts to bubble to prevent it from burning. Add half of the chicken and cook, stirring, for 3–4 minutes or until golden and just cooked through. Transfer to a plate and leave to rest. Wipe out the pan with paper towel. Repeat this process with another 30 g butter, 2 teaspoons olive oil and the remaining chicken.

2   Carefully wipe the pan clean with paper towel and return to the heat. Add the remaining butter and melt until nut-brown, then add the remaining olive oil to prevent it from burning. Add the fennel to the pan and cook for 2–3 minutes or until softened. Deglaze the pan with verjuice, then cook the fennel for a further 1 minute for the verjuice to become syrupy. Add the chicken stock, then simmer over medium–high heat for 5 minutes or until reduced by two-thirds. Add the chicken, preserved lemon and olives and stir to combine well. Remove from the heat and set aside.

3   Preheat the oven griller to medium heat. Brush the pitas with extra olive oil, then place on a baking tray and grill for 2 minutes or until warmed through and light golden, taking care not to overcook as the bread will become too crisp. Remove from the griller and place on a chopping board. Cut the pitas in half crossways and place 5 halves on a chopping board. Stir the parsley into the chicken mixture, then divide evenly among the 5 pita halves and evenly sprinkle over the feta. Season with salt and pepper.

4   Top with the 5 remaining pita halves and return to the oven griller for 2–3 minutes just to warm through. Cut each pita sandwich in half (to make 10 quarters) and serve.

CHICKEN, PRUNE AND LEMON TARTS
WITH PINE-NUT MAYONNAISE

Makes 10

Little tarts are terrific for a drinks party. If you're not up for making the pastry, there are some great pre-baked pastry cases you can buy – but taste one before using them to make a big batch, as you do get what you pay for. You could easily cook the chicken in advance to minimise stress on the day but, truth be told, I do it at the last minute for maximum flavour. The idea for these came from an unlikely place when, two years ago, I spotted a rabbit and prune dish to go in an upmarket deli in Moscow. It was accompanied by what I presumed to be a pine-nut mayonnaise as it looked white and grainy and was scattered with pine nuts. Although I didn't taste it, the idea stayed in my mind. The mayonnaise is very rich, which is why I've used it in these quite delicate small chicken tarts – of course the tarts would be wonderful with rabbit instead.

1 quantity Sour-cream Pastry (see page 100)
30 g unsalted butter
extra virgin olive oil, for cooking
2 × 200 g free-range chicken breast
   fillets, skin-on
sea salt and freshly ground black pepper
zest of 3 lemons, removed in 2 cm-wide
   strips with no bitter white pith
15 prunes, pitted and cut into three
handful mint, thinly sliced
1 tablespoon finely grated lemon zest
roasted pine nuts, to serve

PINE-NUT MAYONNAISE
½ cup (65 g) pine nuts
3 free-range egg yolks
1½ tablespoons verjuice
½ teaspoon Dijon mustard
½ clove garlic, finely chopped
½ teaspoon lemon juice
sea salt
1 cup (250 ml) extra virgin olive oil

1 Preheat the oven to 190°C fan-forced (210°C conventional).

2 Roll out the pastry on a lightly floured workbench until 4 mm thick. Cut out ten 9 cm rounds and use to line 10 lightly greased 6 cm tart tins or ovenproof glass dishes. To blind bake, cut out larger circles of foil and press into the sides of the pastry, then fill with baking beads, beans or rice and bake for 10 minutes.

3 To inhibit the pastry from bubbling, remove the foil and weights, then use a clean tea towel to press down on the pastry shells. Bake for another 5 minutes or until light golden. (If needed, press down again with the tea towel and return to the oven if the pastry isn't completely cooked.) Set aside to cool.

4 Reduce the oven temperature to 180°C fan-forced (200°C conventional).

5 To make the mayonnaise, place the pine nuts on a baking tray and roast for 6–7 minutes or until golden, checking them frequently to make sure they don't burn. Set aside to cool completely. Transfer to a blender and blitz until a fine paste forms.

6 Place the egg yolks and verjuice in a bowl and whisk until pale and creamy. Add the mustard, garlic, lemon juice and ½ teaspoon salt and whisk to combine. Whisk in the olive oil drop by drop at first, and then in a slow but steady stream until the mixture is thick and glossy. Fold in the pine-nut paste until well combined. Cover with plastic film and refrigerate until required. (Makes about 300 ml.)

7 Melt the butter in a frying pan over high heat and cook for 2–3 minutes until nut-brown, adding a splash of olive oil when the butter starts to bubble to prevent it from burning. Season the chicken with salt and pepper and add to the pan with the lemon zest. Cook the chicken, skin-side down, for 5 minutes, then remove the lemon zest strips and set aside. Flip the chicken over and cook for another 5 minutes or until cooked through. Remove the chicken from the pan and leave to cool.

8 Cut the cooled chicken into 1 cm pieces and place in a bowl, then add the prunes and enough of the mayonnaise to bind. Stir in half each of the mint and grated lemon zest, then taste and adjust the seasoning, if necessary.

9 Scoop the chicken mixture evenly into the pastry cases and fill to just above the top of the pastry, then add the reserved lemon zest strips. Sprinkle the tarts with the pine nuts and remaining mint and lemon zest. Serve.

LAMB KIBBEH

Serves 10 as part of a buffet

This is a family favourite and I wonder whether this has its base in my childhood, as I always snaffled a bit of the raw sausage mince when I helped to make rissoles – a tradition that followed first with my children and now grandchildren. The lamb needs to be fresh, sweet and cut without sinew, then kept very chilled until served. When offered with witlof leaves or pita bread alongside for scooping up, it makes wonderful party food with a minimum of work. If you think your guests may be shy of the idea of this, make sure you scatter the fresh herbs right to the edge of the dish to take the edge off the first impression being of raw meat.

4 large green olives
75 g burghul
250 g lamb fillet, sinew removed
1 teaspoon ground cinnamon
1 teaspoon ground allspice
2 spring onions, very thinly sliced
pinch of smoked sweet paprika
sea salt

1 preserved lemon quarter, flesh removed and discarded, rind rinsed and thinly sliced
2 tablespoons mint, thinly sliced
extra virgin olive oil, for drizzling
freshly ground black pepper
4 heads witlof, leaves separated, washed and dried
lemon wedges, to serve

1 Slice off both sides of each olive, then thinly slice and set aside. Discard the pits.

2 Place the burghul in a bowl and pour water over just to cover. Leave to soak for 5 minutes, then squeeze out any excess water.

3 Mince the lamb using the finest mincer attachment (or buy the lamb on the day you are serving this and ask your butcher to do this). Transfer the lamb to a bowl and add the cinnamon, allspice, spring onion, paprika, ½ teaspoon salt and softened burghul and mix well with a wooden spoon. Mince through the mincer once more, if you have one.

4 Transfer the lamb mixture to a flat 30 cm serving dish and pat down to an even thickness. Place the sliced olives and preserved lemon in the centre of the dish and garnish with mint. Drizzle generously with olive oil and season with salt and pepper to taste.

5 Serve the kibbeh with witlof leaves for scooping and lemon wedges for squeezing.

Lemon-glazed
chicken
wings

LEMON-GLAZED
CHICKEN WINGS

Serves 10 as part of a buffet

Who doesn't like chicken wings? Yet, as always, the difference in the quality of your produce will out, so buy wings from a butcher that sells the best chooks you can find. The trick is not to crowd the pan, otherwise the wings will sweat and poach. Whilst I love most food only just cooked, the secret to these wings lies in cooking them until the skin is burnished, which may mean they are really cooked through. However, the fat of this cut saves the wings from being dry. Although you generally serve wings with napkins, I'm not above putting out communal finger bowls for my friends to save on all that extra laundry!

½ cup (180 g) honey, warmed a little

2 tablespoons lemon thyme,
   roughly chopped

1 tablespoon rosemary, finely chopped

¼ cup (60 ml) extra virgin olive oil,
   plus extra for drizzling

zest of 1 lemon, removed in long, thin strips

¼ cup (60 ml) lemon juice

1 tablespoon vino cotto

1 kg chicken wings, tips removed, then
   separated into 2 at the joint

sea salt

1 Place the honey, thyme, rosemary, olive oil, lemon zest and juice and vino cotto in a large bowl and mix well. Add the chicken wings and toss to coat with the marinade, then cover with plastic film and leave to marinate in the fridge for 1 hour.

2 Preheat the oven to as high as it will go – generally 240°C or 250°C (fan-forced and conventional).

3 Drain the marinade from the wings, then pat them dry with paper towel and place on a baking tray. Drizzle with olive oil and season with salt, then roast for 10 minutes or until cooked through and well burnished, turning so as not to burn the herbs in the marinade.

4 Remove the chicken wings from the oven and leave to rest for a few minutes. Drizzle with olive oil and serve.

CHESTNUT AND CHOCOLATE POTS
WITH PINEAPPLE

Serves 10

This is a recipe that began a long time ago in my cooking career and has morphed so many times over the years. This latest incarnation comes from a young chef who presented my recipe at a book-tour function I spoke at a few years ago. His twist of topping the chestnut and chocolate pots with finely diced fresh pineapple delighted me so much I've now written it into the recipe. This works so well as a sweet morsel to serve in small glasses for a stand-up party, although it could easily be made in one big bowl to serve at the centre of your table. The pineapple needs to be prepared close to serving time – or you could always use fresh raspberries instead to counterbalance this rich dessert.

1 × 435 g tin unsweetened chestnut puree
   (such as Sabaton brand, available from
   specialty food stores)
½ cup (125 ml) pouring cream
¼ cup (60 ml) verjuice or water
20 g unsalted butter
1½ tablespoons Cognac
1 tablespoon marmalade
2 teaspoons soft brown sugar

¼ pineapple, peeled, cored and cut into
   8 mm dice

CHOCOLATE GANACHE
⅔ cup (160 ml) pouring cream
120 g dark couverture chocolate
   (70% cocoa solids), roughly chopped
1 teaspoon unsalted butter

1 Place the chestnut puree, cream and verjuice or water in a heavy-based saucepan over low heat, stirring for 5 minutes or until the puree has melted and combined with the cream and verjuice or water. Add the butter and stir until melted, then add the Cognac, marmalade and brown sugar and stir until well combined.

2 Remove the chestnut mixture from the heat, then transfer to a food processor and process until smooth and well combined. Divide evenly among ten 90 ml-capacity glasses and refrigerate for 20 minutes or until chilled and just firm.

3 Meanwhile, to make the chocolate ganache, bring the cream to the boil in a small heavy-based saucepan over medium–high heat. Place the chocolate in a heatproof bowl and pour the boiling cream over. Set aside for 3 minutes to allow the hot cream to melt the chocolate, then give it a gentle stir to combine. Stir in the butter to give the ganache a shiny finish.

4 Divide the warm ganache evenly among the 10 glasses, then set aside at room temperature to cool and set the chocolate.

5 Top with diced pineapple and serve.

Chestnut and
chocolate pots
with pineapple

Christmas Carols Buffet for the Choir

WEDNESDAY NIGHT IS SINGING NIGHT AT MY HOUSE AND, as much as I try not to be away for this, if it absolutely can't be avoided, the 'girls' have a key to let themselves in. We have such a lot of fun singing together just for the joy of it. Over the years, we have grown so much in our abilities, thanks to our teachers along the way. Now with the irrepressible talent of Charmaine Jones, senior jazz lecturer at the Conservatorium of Music, and her sister Jo, both of whom ooze music out of every pore, the choir has lifted another notch. We're put through our paces with gusto, but never to the exclusion of fun. The energy levels of the group are such that, regardless of how exhausted I may be after a difficult day, I'm inevitably flying high by the end of it.

A love of great food comes together with our love of music. When it came to planning this buffet for the choir, I wanted to have as much prepared in advance as possible. I definitely had a helper too, as it's not something I could have pulled off on my own without missing out on the singing. It was such a beautiful night and we were rehearsing in earnest for our carols night at a local church the Sunday before Christmas. And I didn't want to miss any of the work-out, as singing in public is not something we do often.

I planned to serve food at our table underneath the wisteria tree, which I set simply with my array of mismatched plates, forks and napkins. No formal setting here, just a mix of chairs from inside and out, ready to be pulled to the table after setting the food in the centre. Candles were found and put into preserving jars for the evening, when the gully winds had abated enough for us to sit outside. It was worth waiting for darkness to fall to experience being bathed in the gentleness of candlelight. Such feasts require organisation, but the generosity of dishes, bustle of friends helping bring everything to the table, and ensuing frenzy of everyone passing food around and serving themselves, resulted in a successful evening of simple elegance. Then back to the singing, this time with a glass of wine in hand for the final run through, with lots of joy!

I held back on serving the neenish tarts until we'd finished singing, secretly hoping some of my friends would be too full to eat anything else so there'd be more left over for me — very dangerous that! I even forgot to serve the shot glasses of espresso jelly left to set in the garage fridge because I'd run out of room in the kitchen. The moral is: don't let out of sight be out of mind. This is where a big note on the kitchen fridge door, 'Don't forget the jellied coffee in bottom fridge' would have come in handy.

Christmas Carols Buffet for the Choir

Menu for 8

Eggplant salad ~ 96

Pastry slabs with agresto, figs and prosciutto ~ 100

Slow-cooked zucchini ~ 101

Tea-smoked ocean trout with fennel ~ 106

Pickled fig-glazed leg of ham ~ 112

Squid risotto with roasted truss tomatoes ~ 116

Raspberries in sparkling Shiraz jelly ~ 121

Neenish tarts ~ 124

Espresso and Amaretto jellies ~ 126

EGGPLANT SALAD

Serves 8 as an accompaniment

It's a real race every year for me to have grown eggplants in time for the Christmas party season. Whilst I know you can easily buy eggplant from the greengrocers, for those of you who are gardening enthusiasts, I thought I'd share an early-season eggplant variety I've discovered called Eggplant Caspar, featuring totally white skins with creamy flesh – seek out the seeds if you can. Too often I find eggplant that has been undercooked, so the important thing here is to pan-fry the eggplant in batches over a high heat, making sure each slice is well-coloured and cooked through.

1 cup (70 g) coarse fresh sourdough
  breadcrumbs
2 tablespoons extra virgin olive oil, plus
  extra for shallow-frying and drizzling
4 eggplants (aubergines) (about 290 g each),
  cut into 1 cm-thick slices

1 tablespoon vino cotto
2 tablespoons lemon juice
3 tablespoons flat-leaf parsley,
  roughly chopped
zest of 2 lemons, removed in long, thin strips
sea salt and freshly ground black pepper

1 Preheat the oven to 200°C fan-forced (220 °C conventional). Line a baking tray with baking paper.

2 Place the breadcrumbs and olive oil in a bowl and mix together with your hands. Transfer to the prepared tray and bake for 10 minutes or until golden and crisp. Set aside on paper towel to drain and cool.

3 Pour a 5 mm-deep layer of olive oil into a large heavy-based frying pan and heat over high heat. Working in batches so as not to crowd the pan, fry the eggplant for 4–5 minutes on each side or until cooked through and well-coloured all over, adding extra oil to the pan as needed. Remove with tongs and drain on paper towel.

4 Place the eggplant in a large bowl, then drizzle with the vino cotto and lemon juice. Add the parsley and half of the lemon zest, then season to taste with salt and pepper and gently toss to combine. Transfer to a serving dish, then scatter with the breadcrumbs and remaining lemon zest. Serve at room temperature.

Pastry slabs with agresto, figs and prosciutto

PASTRY SLABS WITH AGRESTO, FIGS AND PROSCIUTTO

Serves 8 as part of a buffet

The principle behind this dish is baking the biggest slab of pastry you can fit in your oven (either your own pastry or a quality purchased one, such as my local one made by Carême) early in the day of any party, then topping it with whatever the season inspires. Here I've used the first flush of figs, in tandem with prosciutto and this special type of pesto, made with verjuice to keep it the most vibrant green for several hours after it's made. Perfect for preparing in advance, then assembling just before your guests arrive, this is much easier than making individual tarts, yet just as good to eat.

8 large fresh ripe figs, cut into
   three lengthways
2 tablespoons extra virgin olive oil
1 tablespoon vino cotto
sea salt
100 g very thinly sliced prosciutto
soft herbs, such as micro-basil, to serve

SOUR-CREAM PASTRY
200 g chilled unsalted butter, chopped
250 g plain flour, plus extra for dusting
120 ml sour cream, as needed

AGRESTO
1 clove garlic, peeled
sea salt
4 cups (145 g) firmly packed basil leaves
½ cup (125 ml) extra virgin olive oil
½ cup (80 g) pine nuts
¼ cup (20 g) grated parmesan
freshly ground black pepper
⅓ cup (80 ml) verjuice

1 To make the sour-cream pastry, pulse the butter and flour in a food processor until it resembles coarse breadcrumbs. With the motor running, add ¼ cup (60 ml) of the sour cream and pulse, then add the remaining sour cream, only if necessary, and continue to pulse until the dough just comes together to form a ball. Turn out onto a clean lightly floured workbench and bring it together into a rectangle with your hands. Divide the pastry into two-thirds and one-third. Wrap both pieces in plastic film. Chill the larger piece in the refrigerator for 20 minutes only or it may become too hard to roll. Freeze the other piece for later use.

2 Preheat the oven to 220°C fan-forced (240°C conventional).

3 Roll out the pastry to form a 36 cm × 16 cm rectangle; it may shrink a little when cooked. Lay the pastry on a baking tray and prick it all over with a fork (this is called docking). Bake for 15 minutes or until golden brown. Set aside to cool.

4 To make the agresto, crush the garlic with ½ teaspoon salt by dragging the back of a large knife over it on a chopping board a number of times. Place the basil, olive oil, pine nuts, parmesan, garlic paste, 1 teaspoon salt and pepper to taste in a food processor and blend until amalgamated but it still retains some texture. Add the verjuice and pulse to just combine: this will turn the agresto a brilliant apple-green.

5 Cut the pastry into sixteen 6 cm × 4 cm rectangles. Spread a generous amount of agresto over each pastry rectangle. Place the figs in a bowl and drizzle with the olive oil and vino cotto, then season with salt and divide evenly among the pastry rectangles. Drape the prosciutto over the figs and scatter with soft herbs. Serve.

SLOW-COOKED ZUCCHINI

Serves 8 as an accompaniment

Until my last trip to Italy I would never have eaten zucchini unless it was small and only just cooked. The moment of change came at a restaurant in Rome when I was served a dish of zucchini and beans that had been cooked so long and slow, then drizzled with extra virgin olive oil and served with parmesan. It was an epiphany of taste, so different from eating small, young, quickly cooked zucchini, that I started to leave some of my zucchinis to mature a bit more before picking, particularly when planning to cook for a big group. Whilst this won't thrill your eye in quite the same way as just-cooked zucchini, believe me, it's delicious.

1 kg zucchini (courgettes), cut into
   2 cm-thick slices
sea salt
¼ cup (60 ml) extra virgin olive
   oil, plus extra for drizzling

3 cloves garlic, thinly sliced
⅓ cup (80 ml) verjuice
freshly ground black pepper
3 tablespoons basil leaves
3 tablespoons mint leaves

1 Place the zucchini slices in a single layer on a large wire rack, then sprinkle with 2 tablespoons salt. Leave to stand for 40–60 minutes, then rinse off the salt and dry really well with paper towel, squeezing out any excess moisture.

2 Heat the olive oil in a heavy-based saucepan with a tight-fitting lid over medium heat. Add the garlic and saute for 1 minute or until fragrant, then add the zucchini and stir to coat in the oil. Reduce the heat to low, then cover and cook for 30 minutes. Add the verjuice, then season to taste with salt and pepper. Cover and cook for another 30 minutes or until the zucchini is very soft and meltingly tender; check occasionally and use a simmer mat if the zucchini starts to catch on the base of the pan.

3 Drain the zucchini, if desired, then check and adjust the seasoning, if necessary. Transfer to a large bowl, then scatter with the basil and mint and drizzle with olive oil. Serve warm or at room temperature.

Slow-cooked zucchini

Tea-smoked ocean trout with fennel

TEA-SMOKED OCEAN TROUT
WITH FENNEL

Serves 8–10 as part of a buffet

I prefer ocean trout to salmon due to its tighter texture; however, salmon works equally well in this dish. The type of barbecue you use will give a different result, so keep an eye on the temperature as you don't want the fish to overcook, but at the same time you will need to maintain the heat so the sugar and tea mixture continues to smoke, as this is what not only infuses the fish with flavour, but gives the skin a lovely burnish. (Use a barbecue with a swinging rack, if you have one.) I recommend giving it a go as it's a great way to feed a lot of people at a buffet. The bitter leaf salad on page 253 is an excellent accompaniment. Here, I omitted the grapes and added walnuts and shaved parmesan.

125 g green tea or orange pekoe tea leaves
250 g soft brown sugar
250 g caster sugar
100 ml extra virgin olive oil, plus extra
 for drizzling
1½ small bulbs fennel, very thinly sliced,
 including the fronds
1 × 2.2 kg ocean trout or Atlantic salmon,
 cleaned and scaled

1 orange, sliced
1 lemon, sliced
sea salt and freshly ground black pepper
1 tablespoon lemon juice
micro-mint or small mint leaves and
 lemon slices, to serve (optional)

1 Make 3 rectangular 'boxes' for the smoking mixture using several layers of foil (I make the packages 15 cm × 12 cm to fit under the grill-plate of my barbecue or you can use shallow foil trays available from supermarkets). Combine the tea and sugars and divide the mixture among the foil containers, then set aside.

2 Heat 2 tablespoons of the olive oil in a saucepan over medium heat, then saute the fennel for 5 minutes, stirring occasionally. Stuff the fennel into the cavity of the fish with the orange and lemon. Season the fish with 2 teaspoons salt and a little pepper and moisten it with the remaining olive oil.

3 Place the foil containers under the grill-plate directly over the burners or coals of the barbecue. Oil the barbecue grill-plate and make sure the bars are absolutely clean. Heat the barbecue to medium–high heat and wait for the aroma from the smoking mixture – there will be a strong smell from the sugar caramelising, but it will dissipate quickly. Reduce the barbecue heat to low. Place the fish on the grill-plate, then shut the lid of the barbecue and cook for 5 minutes. Carefully turn the fish over and cook for 5 minutes on the other side. Check the thickest part of the flesh behind the head – it should be moist and a little rare near the bone. Turn off the heat and leave the fish in the covered barbecue for 2 minutes for medium–rare or until cooked

to your liking. (Heat builds up quickly in these barbecues and the thermometer may climb as high as 200°C. If this happens, turn the fish over and turn the heat off, then leave for another 6 minutes or until rare in the centre near the bone. If your barbecue has a swinging rack, then place the fish on this and leave to rest in the turned off barbecue for another 10 minutes.)

4 Transfer the fish to a large platter or baking tray and set aside to rest until cool enough to handle. Carefully remove the skin, then drizzle with olive oil and the lemon juice and season with salt. Serve the fish warm or at room temperature, sprinkled with micro-mint or small mint leaves and lemon slices, if desired.

pickled fig-glazed

eg of ham

PICKLED FIG-GLAZED LEG OF HAM

Serves 16–20 as part of a buffet

What a tradition this is in my family, starting with early memories of Mum boiling a ham in the copper – an age before my daughter Saskia started her Black Pig range of local Berkshire pig products. Now that Saskia's products are so close to hand it's amazing how often I find I can use a glazed leg of ham at the centre of the table. Just recently, I've glazed a leg of ham for: a post-wedding brunch party; the choir singing at the 11 am timeslot at the Barossa markets, after which everyone is ravenous; a staff information night at the Farmshop; and a wine tasting where I wanted to ensure I offered something substantial. A slice or two of ham with some good local bread and pickles alongside is so simple to prepare yet it makes such a statement. Whatever size leg of ham you buy, the process of glazing (see photographs on previous pages) will still be the same – simply reduce the cooking time for a smaller leg.

1 × 7 kg leg of ham, traditionally smoked
cloves (optional), as needed
1 cup (250 ml) water, plus extra as needed

PICKLED FIG GLAZE
1 tablespoon vino cotto
¼ cup (70 g) Dijon mustard
2 × 360 g jars Maggie Beer Pickled Figs
(available from maggiebeer.com.au),
cut in half crossways, plus ¼ cup (60 ml)
of the pickling syrup

1 Take the ham out of the fridge and leave for 1 hour to come to room temperature (this also makes it easier to strip off the skin).

2 Preheat the oven to its highest heat setting – usually 240°C or 250°C (fan-forced or conventional).

3 Strip the leathery skin from the ham, being careful not to remove any fat from underneath – you are after a 5 mm–1 cm layer of fat. Score the fat quite deeply into a diamond pattern, taking care not to cut through to the meat. The size of the diamonds should suit the size of the fruit you will use to decorate.

4 To make the pickled fig glaze, mix the vino cotto, mustard and ¼ cup (60 ml) of the pickled fig syrup into a paste and rub half the mixture over the top and sides of the ham.

5 Place the ham in a roasting pan on a trivet covered with baking paper, add ½ cup (125 ml) of the water to the pan and bake for 8 minutes. Brush the ham with some of the remaining fig glaze, then turn the pan around and bake for another 20 minutes. You are looking for a good even burnish over the fat (if it starts to burn, add a little more water to the pan).

6 Remove the pan from the oven, then brush more glaze over the ham. Place the fig halves on the diamond shapes and carefully hold them in place with toothpicks or cloves, then brush the remaining glaze over the figs.

7 Reduce the oven temperature to 220°C fan-forced (240°C conventional). Add the remaining water to the pan to prevent the pan juices from burning. Bake the ham for another 15 minutes or until it is beautifully glazed, then leave to cool.

8 Proudly place the glazed ham at the centre of your table, then cut into slices and serve.

9 To store the leftover ham, put a reasonable amount of cold water in a large bowl in the sink and add ¼ cup (60 ml) white vinegar. Rinse a clean pillow case, calico flour bag or large tea towel in the water and vinegar mixture, making sure it is totally wet. Wring it out well, taking care that it is still moist, then wrap the ham inside. Repeat this with a clean pillow case, calico bag or tea towel every couple of days and the ham will easily keep in the fridge for up to 10 days.

Squid risotto with roasted truss tomatoes

SQUID RISOTTO WITH ROASTED TRUSS TOMATOES

Serves 8 as part of a buffet or 4 as a main

This is a dish I make often and I've written it down before, but each time I add a different flourish or two – here in the form of bright red tomatoes. I know of no better way to feed a crowd than preparing a huge risotto in my enormous paella pan on the wok burner in my courtyard. I often make it in front of my guests, getting them to take turns stirring it as I add the ingredients. Squid risotto is my favourite of all, as much for the drama of the colour – as well as flavour – of the black ink-infused rice. I've often served this to people who've recoiled at the thought of squid ink, yet who, without exception, have loved it upon tasting. If you're lucky enough to find whole squid with the ink sacs intact, you won't need to buy the squid ink sachets listed below. You could make this a little easier by adding the squid directly to the rice in the last stages of cooking, in which case, cut the squid down the centre, then into thin strips rather than rings.

1.5 litres fish stock, plus extra if needed
100 g unsalted butter, chopped
2 tablespoons extra virgin olive oil,
   plus extra for drizzling
1 onion, finely chopped
3 cloves garlic, finely chopped
2 cups (400 g) arborio rice
½ cup (125 ml) verjuice
sea salt
zest of 1 lemon, removed in wide strips
   with no bitter white pith
3 × 4 g sachets squid ink (available
   from fishmongers and specialty food
   stores) (optional)
freshly ground black pepper
finely grated zest of 2 lemons
lots of roughly chopped flat-leaf parsley
   and lemon wedges, to serve

PAN-FRIED SQUID

1 kg squid (ink sacs intact if possible)
⅔ cup (100 g) plain flour
sea salt and freshly ground black pepper
60 g unsalted butter, plus extra if needed
extra virgin olive oil, for cooking
juice of 2 lemons

ROASTED TRUSS TOMATOES

12 small vine-ripened truss tomatoes,
   cut into halves crossways, leaving
   stems intact
2 tablespoons extra virgin olive oil
sea salt and freshly ground black pepper

1 To roast the tomatoes, preheat the oven to 100°C fan-forced (120°C conventional). Place the tomatoes, cut-side up, on a baking tray lined with baking paper. Drizzle with the olive oil and season to taste with salt and pepper. Roast for 1 hour or until cooked through and almost collapsed. Set aside to cool.

2 To prepare the squid, remove the ink sacs, if intact, and set them aside (the silvery sac is quite hard and located between the eyes – be careful that you don't pierce it). Reserve 2 of the ink sacs and discard the remainder. Cut the tentacles away from the heads and set aside. Remove the hard quill from the middle of each squid tube and discard. Clean out each tube using a long-handled spoon and discard the innards. Strip away and discard the purplish-black outer membrane. Run the tubes under cold water, then pat dry with paper towel. Cut the tentacles into bite-sized pieces and the tubes into 8 mm-thick rings.

3 Bring the stock to the boil in a saucepan over high heat and keep warm.

4 Meanwhile, melt the butter with the olive oil in a large deep heavy-based frying pan over medium heat. Add the onion, then saute for 5 minutes or until softened and translucent. Reduce the heat to low and add the garlic, then gently cook for 2 minutes.

5 Increase the heat to medium–high and add the rice, stirring well until each grain is coated in the butter and oil mixture. Make a well in the centre of the rice mixture, then increase the heat to high and add the verjuice with a whoosh and give the mixture a quick stir until the verjuice has evaporated. Add salt to taste (I use 1½ teaspoons). Reduce the heat to medium and add the stock to the rice mixture, a ladleful at a time, stirring continuously and waiting for each addition to be absorbed before adding the next.

6 When you have used one-quarter of the stock, add the lemon zest strips. Continue adding the stock a ladleful at a time, adding the ink sachets or reserved sacs with the last ladleful of stock and stirring carefully so as not to break up the lemon zest. Continue to cook until the rice is al dente and the mixture is thick and syrupy: the whole cooking time should be about 20 minutes. Add a generous drizzle of olive oil, then season to taste with pepper and add extra salt, if desired. Keep warm.

7 To cook the squid, working in 3 batches, toss the squid rings in the seasoned flour, then shake in a colander to remove any excess flour. Melt 20 g of the butter in a large heavy-based frying pan over high heat until it sizzles, then add a splash of olive oil to prevent it from burning. Toss one-third of the squid into the hot pan and cook for 1 minute on each side or until it just starts to turn white. Drain the squid on paper towel, then drizzle with one-third of the lemon juice. Wipe the pan clean with paper towel and repeat another two times with the remaining butter, olive oil, squid and lemon juice.

8 Stir the grated lemon zest and parsley into the risotto, then spoon the risotto onto a platter and top with the squid and roasted tomatoes. Drizzle any roasted tomato juices and a little olive oil over the top. Serve with lemon wedges alongside.

Raspberries
in Sparkling
Shiraz
Jelly

RASPBERRIES IN
SPARKLING SHIRAZ JELLY

Serves 8

So many food traditions in my family come from my earliest memories, yet this one began about 15 years ago after I dined at the Art Gallery Restaurant in Adelaide. The chef, Cath Kerry, served a wine jelly, possibly with raspberries, but my memory isn't clear so I can't be sure. I loved it so much I took the idea a step further by using sparkling Shiraz, which adds a spicy character. I must admit to being extravagant at times with the amount of raspberries I set in this jelly, but you can use as few or as many as you like. The important thing is to burn off the alcohol, not only so that you can share the jelly with children, but also to give it the best possible flavour. The jelly will only be as good as the quality of your Shiraz, so splash out!

1 × 750 ml bottle sparkling Shiraz
200 g caster sugar
8 × 2 g gold-strength gelatine leaves (for
  a firm set in case of very hot weather)

2 cups (500 ml) cold water
450 g raspberries (choose the very best
  you can find)
Jersey cream or double cream, to serve

1 Place the wine and caster sugar in a stainless-steel saucepan and bring to the boil, then light a match and carefully touch it to the surface to burn off the alcohol. Turn off the heat and stir until the sugar has dissolved.

2 Meanwhile, soften the gelatine leaves in a bowl with the cold water for 5 minutes. Drain the softened leaves and gently squeeze to remove excess water, then add immediately to the wine mixture and stir whilst still hot to dissolve the gelatine. Set aside to cool completely.

3 Place the raspberries in a 1 litre-capacity glass serving bowl and slowly pour the cooled wine mixture over them so it doesn't froth. The raspberries will rise to the surface so gently press down on them with a spoon to ensure they absorb enough liquid to set in the top of the jelly. Cover with plastic film, then refrigerate overnight to set.

4 I generally serve the jelly straight from the bowl. However, if you decide to turn it out, dip the base of the bowl in hot water, then invert the jelly over a large plate. Serve the jelly with Jersey or double cream alongside.

Neenish
tarts

NEENISH TARTS

Makes 15–18 small tarts, depending on the size of the tart shells

How often my childhood memories influence what I make. When I was young, Mum and I had a special tradition of buying a neenish tart each from a bakery on the rare occasions we went shopping in the city. As small and as sweet as neenish tarts are, I have never found one that compares to those from our expeditions – until I decided to make them myself. I've always been scathing about 'mock' cream, although I'm not now that I make it like this. I admit these are fiddly to make, so I must confess that I only make them when I know there will be enough people to eat them all, otherwise I'd finish them off and make myself sick.

2½ tablespoons Maggie Beer Raspberry and Pomegranate Jam or Seville Marmalade (available from maggiebeer.com.au) or your favourite jam

DAMIEN PIGNOLET'S PATE BRISEE
240 g plain flour
pinch of salt
180 g unsalted butter, cut into small pieces, removed from the fridge 30 minutes before using, plus extra softened butter for greasing
¼ cup (60 ml) iced mineral water

LEMON ICING
1 cup (160 g) icing sugar
2 tablespoons lemon juice

CHOCOLATE ICING
1 cup (160 g) icing sugar
2 teaspoons unsweetened cocoa powder
2 tablespoons milk, or as needed

BUTTERCREAM
1½ tablespoons full-cream milk
½ cup (110 g) caster sugar
¼ cup (60 ml) water, plus
    1½ tablespoons hot water
½ teaspoon gelatine powder
180 g unsalted butter, chopped
1 teaspoon finely grated lemon zest

1 Preheat the oven to 190°C fan-forced (210°C conventional). Lightly brush 18 gem tray moulds with softened butter (or use 15 ovenproof Chinese tea cups placed upside-down on a baking tray and lightly brushed with olive oil).

2 To make the pastry, sift the flour and salt onto a clean workbench. Scatter the butter over the flour and toss together using a pastry scraper or cook's knife. Sprinkle with the mineral water and toss again. Gather the flour mixture to the front of the workbench. Using the heel of your hand, smear the ingredients away from you in a quick, smooth sliding action. Gather the emerging dough back to the starting point and repeat the smearing action – this technique is called fraisage (literally, 'kneading'). Do not be concerned if little bits of butter are visible in the dough; this indicates that the pastry has not been overworked. Lightly knead the dough, then form into a disc and wrap in baking paper. Chill in the fridge for 20 minutes only or the pastry may become too hard to roll.

3 Roll the pastry out on a lightly floured workbench to 2–3 mm thick. Cut out eighteen 9 cm rounds and use to line the prepared gem tray (or cut out fifteen 10 cm rounds, then press over the greased upturned tea cups, if using). Cut out larger rounds of foil and press into the pastry in the gem tray, then fill with baking beads, beans or rice and put into the oven for 10 minutes to blind bake (15 minutes if using tea cups). To inhibit the pastry from bubbling, remove the foil and beans, then use a clean tea towel to press down on the pastry shells. Bake for another 5 minutes or until golden and crisp. Press down again with the tea towel if needed (return to the oven again to bake if the pastry isn't completely cooked). Set aside to cool.

4 To make the lemon icing, combine the icing sugar and lemon juice in a bowl to make a smooth, thick, runny paste. For the chocolate icing, in another bowl combine the sugar, cocoa and as much milk as needed to make a smooth, thick, runny paste. Set aside.

5 To make the buttercream, combine the milk, sugar and the ¼ cup (60 ml) water in a bowl and stir until the sugar has dissolved. In a small bowl, sprinkle the gelatine over the 1½ tablespoons hot water, then stir to dissolve and set aside to cool. Stir the gelatine mixture into the milk mixture. Beat the butter in the bowl of an electric mixer for 10 minutes or until light and white, then, with the motor running, gradually add the gelatine and milk mixture. Continue to beat for 12–15 minutes; the mixture will look like it has split, but it will eventually incorporate. Add the lemon zest at the last moment and beat to just combine.

6 Spoon a little jam onto the base of each tart case, then fill each case to the top with buttercream, spreading it evenly across to smooth the surface. Spoon ½–¾ teaspoon of lemon icing over one half of each tart, then spoon ½–¾ teaspoon of the chocolate icing over the other half. Give each tart a little shake to join the 2 icings together.

7 Serve. (Leftover tarts can be stored in an airtight container in the fridge for up to 3 days.)

ESPRESSO AND
AMARETTO JELLIES

Serves 8

It is the Italian custom to finish a meal with little shots of espresso, and I have waited a long time to use the idea of taking this a step further by serving little shot glasses of espresso jelly instead. I first tried this at the Ravida Olive Oil Company and Cooking School in Sicily during an International Olive Oil Council olive grove tour I attended with my friend Stephanie Alexander. It was in the days before espresso machines were prevalent anywhere other than in commercial outlets, and I thought it such a clever way to serve coffee to a large group of people. Even now, with espresso machines more common at home, serving 30 coffees at once is unthinkable, so try this instead.

1 cup (250 ml) freshly made espresso coffee
   shots or best-quality strong plunger coffee
¼ cup (55 g) soft brown sugar
2 × 2 g gold-strength gelatine leaves

2 cups (500 ml) cold water
1½ teaspoons Amaretto
¼ cup (60 ml) Jersey or double cream or
   creme fraiche

1 Heat 150 ml of the coffee gently in a small saucepan over low heat. Add the sugar and stir to dissolve. Heat to just below simmering point, then remove from the heat. Place the gelatine leaves in a bowl with the cold water for 5 minutes or until softened, then squeeze out the excess water. Add immediately to the warm coffee mixture and stir well until the gelatine has dissolved.

2 Immediately pour the gelatine mixture into the remaining coffee and mix well, then add the Amaretto. Divide evenly among 8 serving glasses, then refrigerate for 3 hours or until set.

3 Put a tiny dollop of cream onto each jelly. Serve with teaspoons.

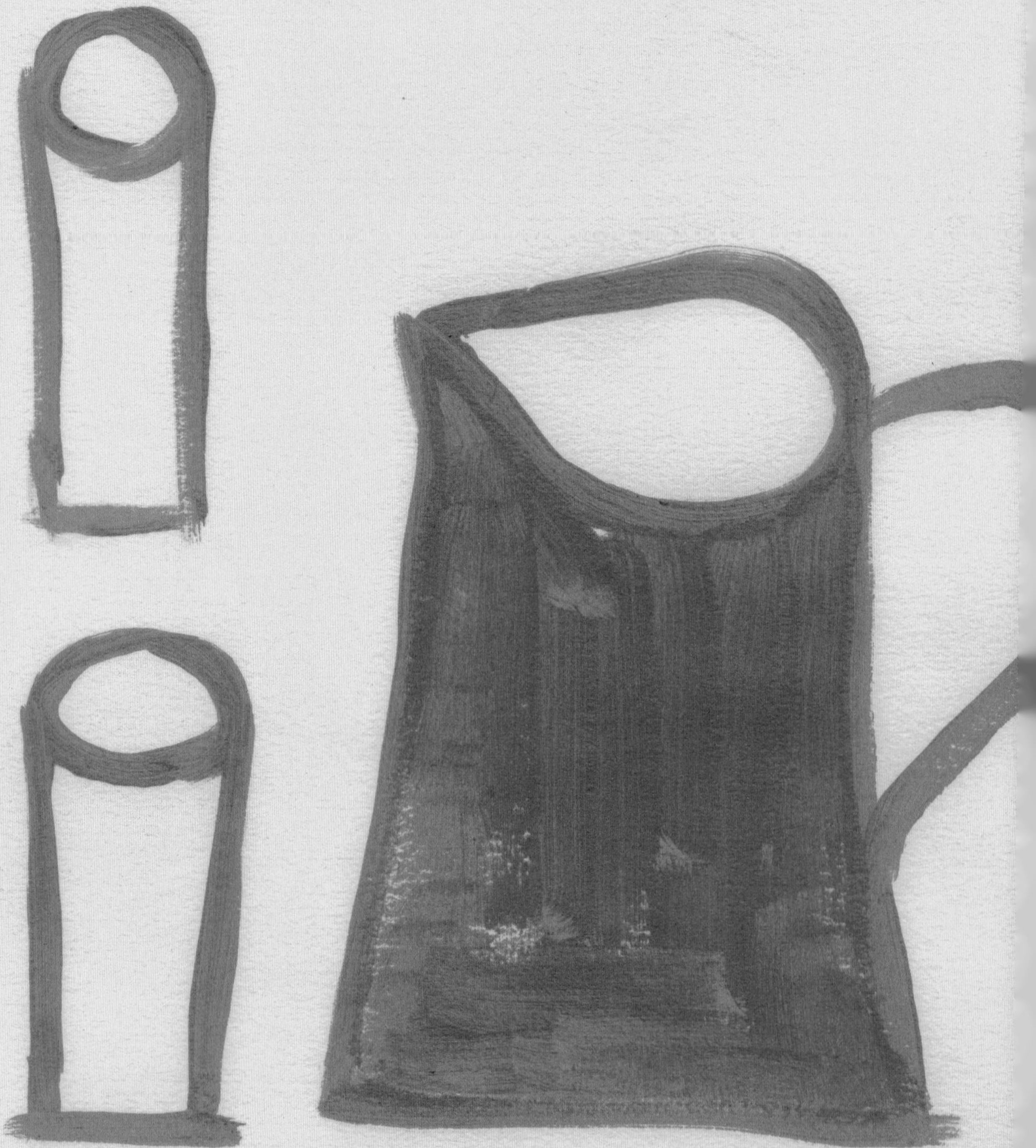

Christmas Eve Supper

I ALWAYS PLAN A SUPPER FOR CHRISTMAS EVE. I NEVER QUITE know whether friends as well as family will drop by, so I need a menu that can expand or contract without anything being wasted. Having done so much cooking earlier in the day ready for Christmas lunch itself, I add a list of simple supper foods that lend themselves to either being put onto the table all at once, or served in stages, so the youngest grandchild can be fed in time to go home for an early night – otherwise the pre-Christmas excitement can get out of control! Again, it's all about planning to ensure the day's cooking agenda is manageable – and preferably you've roped someone in to help.

My priority on this day is getting the big preparations for Christmas Day out of the way, such as making the clotted cream on page 198 in time for it to set. This is where dishes like caponata (see page 146) come into their own, as it's easy to make a big batch to cater for extra guests, but it also works brilliantly packed into airtight containers for leftovers. I keep a stash of 1 litre-capacity takeaway containers with tight-fitting lids in my bottom kitchen drawer for just this eventuality. I am proud to say the corn cobs come from my garden so I only pick them as I need them.

The buttered walnuts on page 140 are done in a moment or two, so if visitors arrive in waves you can cook these in batches and keep them coming. The eggplant with buffalo haloumi on page 141 can be prepped, then cooked a la minute, and the fattoush on page 149 is very last moment too, I agree. However, the quail and chicken can be cooked in advance and served at room temperature, with any remnants tightly covered and refrigerated, making a welcome cold lunch a few days later. Once cured, the ocean trout on page 145 lasts for a good week in the fridge. Leftovers are much-loved sliced thickly and accompanied by scrambled eggs for breakfast, or sliced thinly and served with perfectly ripe avocado on bruschetta for lunch, or pulled out as a nibble to accompany drinks on any of the following nights.

My idea is to make it an early night for all, as we're often still wrapping presents just before going to bed. I have a selection of Christmas music, from classical and jazz to pop, depending on the mood or who is still there. Then, after everyone has gone home, Colin and I share a nightcap of eggnog (if there is any left), listen to carols and wrap the remaining presents, relishing this special, gentle time before the family get-together the next day, and all the excitement of the grandchildren it brings with it.

Christmas Eve Supper

Menu for 8

Eggnog ~ 136

Buttered walnuts with rosemary ~ 140

Eggplant with buffalo haloumi ~ 141

Dill-cured ocean trout with horseradish cream ~ 145

Caponata ~ 146

Fattoush ~ 149

Barbecued corn on the cob ~ 150

Roast quail with figs and bacon and parmesan polenta ~ 152

Baked chicken thighs with preserved lemon and rosemary ~ 157

Roasted almond jelly with cherry compote ~ 158

EGGNOG

Serves 8

There are Barossa families who go to church at midnight on Christmas Eve, then make eggnog to enjoy as they unwrap their presents upon their return home. Whilst the tradition of making eggnog comes from colder parts of the world, there is something so Christmas-y about it that I happily embrace it, but my twist is to serve it super-chilled. Given the large splash of brandy, this recipe is one just for the adults, although you could always pour some off for the children before adding the brandy.

8 free-range egg yolks
125 g caster sugar
2 cups (500 ml) milk
ice cubes

2 cups (500 ml) chilled double cream
⅓ cup (80 ml) brandy
grated or ground nutmeg, to taste

1 Whisk the egg yolks and caster sugar together in a bowl until pale and thick. Warm the milk in a saucepan over low heat until just hot, then slowly whisk into the egg yolk mixture in a slow, steady stream, whisking continuously.

2 Pour the egg yolk mixture into the pan. Return the pan to very low heat and cook, stirring continuously with a wooden spoon, for 3 minutes or until the mixture coats the back of the spoon; do not let it simmer or it may curdle. (Be careful not to overcook the egg or it will scramble; have a bowl of ice alongside the stove in case you need to quickly cool the mixture down.) Immediately pour the eggnog through a coarse-mesh strainer into a heatproof bowl. Stir in the cream, then stir in the brandy. Pour into a serving jug and serve warm or chilled. Add nutmeg to taste.

Buttered walnuts with rosemary

Eggplant with buffalo haloumi

BUTTERED WALNUTS WITH ROSEMARY

Serves 8 as a starter

What nut wouldn't be wonderful cooked with fresh rosemary and butter? Walnuts are particularly delicious prepared like this, but they need to be fresh. My tip is to buy walnuts from a reliable source. I order 3 kg at a time from a small Riverland organic grower, then refrigerate them as soon as they arrive. In Adelaide, fresh walnuts are readily available from The Persian Grocer; they respect quality so much they sell their walnuts from the refrigerator, which is where nuts should be kept (although it's only here I've ever seen it so). If you suspect the walnuts you've bought are rancid, roast them in a 200°C fan-forced (220°C conventional) oven for a few minutes first, then rub off the skins in a clean tea towel as this will remove the 'off' taste and bring out their oils.

100 g unsalted butter, chopped
2 teaspoons extra virgin olive oil

4 tablespoons rosemary leaves
¾ cup (75 g) new-season walnuts

1 Melt the butter in a large frying pan over high heat and cook for 2–3 minutes until nut-brown, adding the olive oil when the butter starts to bubble to prevent it from burning. Add the rosemary and cook for 1–2 minutes or until it changes colour. Add the walnuts and toss to coat well in the butter mixture for 1–2 minutes, taking care not to burn. Serve warm.

EGGPLANT WITH BUFFALO HALOUMI

Serves 8 as a starter

Here I've used the wonderful buffalo haloumi from Trevor Hart in Queensland. As I mention on page 308, when I tried it, it was like no haloumi I'd eaten before, even when compared to the top imported ones. However, just like cooking any haloumi, the trick is to cook it over a lower temperature so that it turns golden on each side without becoming rubbery. Mind you, this haloumi is so excellent it has never got to that rubbery stage, and even tastes great when eaten raw.

olive oil spray, for cooking
2 eggplants (aubergines), tops removed,
   cut lengthways into 5 mm-thick slices
   (about 500 g)
100 ml extra virgin olive oil

¼ cup (60 ml) verjuice
430 g buffalo or other good-quality haloumi,
   cut into 1.5 cm-thick slices
plain flour, for dusting
sea salt and freshly ground black pepper

1 Preheat the oven to 220°C fan-forced (240°C conventional).

2 Spray a baking tray with olive oil spray. Lay the eggplant slices on the tray. Combine ¼ cup (60 ml) of the olive oil and the verjuice in a bowl. Brush the eggplant with the olive oil mixture, then roast for 8 minutes or until burnished. Remove from the oven and quickly turn over, then roast for another 6 minutes or until burnished and cooked through. Set aside.

3 Pat the haloumi dry with paper towel and toss in the seasoned flour, shaking off the excess. Heat the remaining olive oil in a large heavy-based frying pan over medium heat until hot, then pan-fry the haloumi in batches for 2 minutes on each side or until golden.

4 Serve the eggplant and haloumi at once.

Eggnog

Dill-cured ocean trout with horseradish cream

DILL-CURED OCEAN TROUT WITH HORSERADISH CREAM

Serves 16–20 as part of a buffet

This is such a tried-and-true family favourite that it makes an appearance whenever there is even a hint of a get-together. We love it so much that we often buy a whole fish already filleted with the pin-bones removed, then cure both sides at the same time and seal the second piece with my cryovac machine (purchased for about $125 from my local hardware store), to enjoy at our next gathering. Happily, given my daughters and grandchildren all live close by in the Barossa, there are lots of such opportunities. It's a personal choice whether you carve the ocean trout very thinly or more generously. I slice it thinly to serve as a nibble when guests arrive, and a little thicker if serving it as an entree.

1 cup (220 g) caster sugar
1 cup (225 g) table salt
handful dill, finely chopped
1 × 1.3 kg ocean trout fillet
(35 cm long × 13 cm wide × 2 cm thick),
skin-off and pin-boned

HORSERADISH CREAM
1 cup (250 ml) thickened cream
¼ cup (70 g) minced fresh horseradish or
horseradish cream (available in jars from
specialty food stores)

1 Combine the caster sugar, salt and dill in a bowl and mix well.

2 Spread half of the sugar mixture over the base of a clean plastic or enamel tray. Lay the trout on the sugar mixture, then spread the remaining sugar mixture over the top. Cover the trout with a piece of plastic film or baking paper, then place a chopping board or another plastic or enamel tray on top and weight it down with heavy objects (such as tins of food) on top. Refrigerate the trout for 8 hours for a soft cure or for 24 hours for a firmer cure.

3 To make the horseradish cream, place the cream in a glass or stainless-steel bowl. Using hand-held electric beaters, whip the cream until soft peaks form, then fold through the horseradish until well combined. Transfer to a clean bowl, cover with plastic film and refrigerate until required. (Makes about 1¼ cups [310 ml].)

4 After curing, brush all the salt mixture off the trout, using the back of a knife. Thinly slice the trout crossways, then serve with horseradish cream. (Leftovers can be stored in the fridge for up to 3 days.)

CAPONATA

The success of this dish depends on the type of eggplant you use. If you're buying them rather than growing your own, look for small to medium-sized, shiny, dark eggplant, as often the larger, more voluptuous ones have been left on the vine past their perfect maturity. Whilst it may seem more time consuming, it is worth cooking the onion, eggplant and celery separately, then combining them at the end with the other ingredients and a little bit of dark chocolate, which adds a subtle extra dimension to the dish without being overpowering. This is so versatile – it works as part of a buffet, as a side dish for barbecued lamb, or as a satisfying vegetarian meal, topped with torn fior di latte.

145 ml extra virgin olive oil,
  plus extra as needed
1 onion, roughly chopped
2 tablespoons raw sugar
⅔ cup (160 ml) white wine vinegar
2 (about 530 g) eggplants (aubergines),
  cut into 2 cm pieces
sea salt
2 sticks celery and some young leaves,
  thickly sliced

4 roma (plum) tomatoes, seeded and diced
8 large green olives, pitted and
  roughly chopped
⅓ cup (65 g) baby capers, rinsed and drained
freshly ground black pepper
3 g good-quality dark chocolate,
  finely chopped
large handful basil leaves,
  roughly shredded

1 Heat 1 tablespoon of the olive oil in a large heavy-based frying pan over medium heat. Add the onion and saute for 2 minutes or until it colours a little. Add the sugar and mix well to combine, then deglaze the pan with the vinegar and continue to cook for 5 minutes or until a little syrupy; you should have about 2 tablespoons liquid. Transfer the onion mixture to a bowl and set aside. Wipe the pan clean with paper towel.

2 Heat ¼ cup (60 ml) of the olive oil in the pan over medium–high heat. Fry half of the eggplant for 10 minutes or until deep-golden and almost cooked through, adding a little more oil to the pan, if needed, and a little salt. Transfer to a bowl and repeat with the remaining olive oil and eggplant. Return the eggplant to the pan, then add the celery and toss to mix. Add the tomato, then reduce the heat to low and continue to cook for another 5 minutes or until the tomato has softened a little. Return the onion mixture and any of its liquid to the pan and mix well, then add the olives and capers and season to taste with salt and pepper. Remove from the heat.

3 Immediately add the chocolate to the warm caponata, gently stirring so it melts. Add the basil and adjust the seasoning if necessary – the caponata should be sweet, sour and luscious! Serve warm or at room temperature. (Leftover caponata can be stored in an airtight container in the fridge for up to 3 days.)

FATTOUSH

The freshness of this salad just sings summer flavour and simplicity. It's a great example of how much our multicultural population has added to our Anglo-Saxon ways. The trick here is to use herbs from your own garden, if you can. The difference in flavour is so overwhelming that another thing I urge of you is to start your own herb garden, if you haven't done so already. To ensure the pita bread is crisp, pan-fry it at the last moment, then toss it into the salad just before serving. It's another salad that extends beautifully with the addition of Persian feta or your favourite goat's curd.

4 ripe tomatoes, cut into bite-sized chunks
4 Lebanese cucumbers, peeled and cut
   into bite-sized chunks
2 golden shallots, thinly sliced
2 large handfuls flat-leaf parsley,
   roughly chopped
handful mint, roughly chopped
sea salt
extra virgin olive oil, for pan-frying
2 small round flatbreads or pita breads

SUMAC DRESSING
2 cloves garlic, very finely chopped
2 teaspoons ground sumac
⅓ cup (80 ml) lemon juice
½ cup (125 ml) extra virgin olive oil
sea salt and freshly ground black pepper

1 Place the tomato, cucumber, shallot, parsley and mint in a large bowl and mix. Season with a little salt and set aside.

2 To make the dressing, combine the garlic, sumac, lemon juice and olive oil in a small bowl and season to taste with salt and pepper. Pour half of the dressing over the salad, then set aside for at least 10 minutes to allow the flavours to infuse.

3 Just before serving, add a splash of olive oil to a large heavy-based frying pan over medium–high heat. Tear the flatbread into bite-sized pieces, then pan-fry in batches for 1½–2 minutes or until golden and crisp.

4 Immediately toss the fried flatbread through the salad, add a little more dressing and serve at once.

BARBECUED CORN ON THE COB

Serves 8 as an accompaniment

This corn, of course, came direct from my garden. Okay, I am bragging a little, but the taste of just-picked and cooked corn is unbeatable, and one that my grandchildren just love. The interesting thing about corn is that it's one vegetable where hybridisation has increased the flavour to counteract the loss that occurs during transportation and storage. Even so, freshly picked corn will always be the best. It's up to your conscience whether you serve it with lashings of butter or extra virgin olive oil – both are wonderful – plus salt flakes, and fresh herbs, if you want it to be a little fancy.

8 cobs fresh corn, husks on
extra virgin olive oil, for brushing
200 g unsalted butter

1 Preheat a barbecue grill-plate to high.

2 Strip back the husk from each corn cob, discarding the husks. Brush each cob with olive oil, then grill on each side for 3–4 minutes or until lightly charred and cooked, brushing with extra oil each time the cobs are turned.

3 Generously rub the butter over each corn cob and serve.

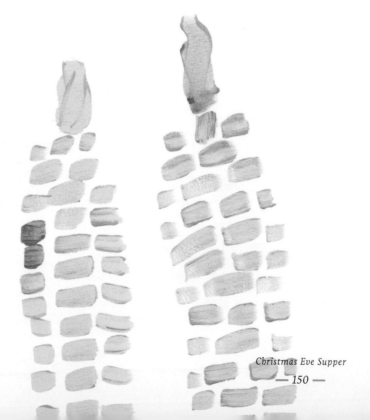

ROAST QUAIL WITH FIGS AND BACON
AND PARMESAN POLENTA

Serves 8 as a main

I love quail, either roasted, barbecued or pan-fried, and I always eat it with my fingers, whether I'm at home or in a restaurant. It's best of all when the skin is nicely burnished, and this marriage with fresh figs is my favourite combination of all. I learnt from experience, a bad one at that, if you stuff the quail with the figs the night before they will break down the meat, making it mushy. I share this to say that preparing in advance doesn't always work. I enjoy soft polenta in any season, and it is a great option for the vegetarian in the family – just put some aside in a separate bowl with lots of butter and extra virgin olive oil, to be enjoyed alongside something else from the table, then serve the rest with the quail.

8 grape leaves (optional)
8 figs, cut in half lengthways
2 tablespoons extra virgin olive oil,
  plus extra for drizzling
1 tablespoon lemon thyme leaves
finely grated zest of 1 lemon
8 × 220 g jumbo quail, removed from
  the fridge 30 minutes before cooking
sea salt and freshly ground black pepper
30 g unsalted butter
130 g belly bacon, rind removed and cut
  into 8 slices (if unavailable, use 8 rashers
  streaky bacon, rind removed)

⅓ cup (80 ml) verjuice
roughly chopped flat-leaf parsley,
  to serve

PARMESAN POLENTA
1.5 litres full-cream milk
sea salt
1 cup (180 g) polenta
1 cup (80 g) grated parmesan
freshly ground white pepper

1 Preheat the oven to 220°C fan-forced (240°C conventional). Place the grape leaves (if using) on a baking tray and set aside.

2 Place half the figs in a bowl, then drizzle with a little olive oil and add the lemon thyme and lemon zest. Stuff each quail cavity evenly with this mixture. Tuck the wings of each quail behind the bird. Rub the quail skin with a little olive oil and season with salt and pepper.

3 Melt the butter in a heavy-based frying pan over high heat and cook for 2–3 minutes until nut-brown, adding the olive oil when the butter starts to bubble to prevent it from burning. Reduce the heat to low–medium, then very gently seal the quail on all sides for 8 minutes, turning until just light-golden all over. Place the quail, breast-side up, on top of the grape leaves (if using) on the baking tray, then put a slice of bacon over each quail breast and place the remaining figs on the tray.

4 Roast the quail for 6–8 minutes or until just cooked. To test if the quail are cooked, pull away one of the legs and check that it is pink but not raw at the joint; return to the oven to cook further if necessary. Immediately turn the quail upside-down and drizzle with the verjuice, then leave to rest for a few minutes.

5 Meanwhile, to make the polenta, place the milk and 2 teaspoons salt in a large heavy-based saucepan over high heat. Bring to a simmer, stirring every couple of minutes to prevent the milk from catching on the base of the pan. Reduce the heat to low–medium. Stirring continuously, gradually pour in the polenta in a steady stream so that no lumps form, stirring until it is all incorporated. Stirring constantly, cook for 5 minutes or until the polenta has thickened but is still slightly sloppy. Stir in the parmesan and pepper to taste, then remove from the heat. (If the polenta stands for 10 minutes or more after removing it from the heat, stir in a small amount of milk, butter or olive oil to moisten it to the desired loose consistency.)

6 Scatter each quail with parsley, then serve on a bed of polenta with the resting juices spooned over and the figs alongside.

Roast quail
with figs and bacon
and parmesan
polenta

BAKED CHICKEN THIGHS WITH PRESERVED LEMON AND ROSEMARY

Serves 8 as part of a buffet or 4 as a main

Whilst this dish was originally geared towards appealing to the grandchildren, it is one the whole family loves. And even if the youngest grandchild is going through an 'I don't eat green' stage, it's easy to quickly pull off the offending bits of rosemary and not add the parsley. This is a great dish to pull together for Christmas Eve, when there are still many jobs to be done in readiness for Christmas Day. Just throw everything onto a baking tray, then put it into the oven and give the tray a shake every now and then. You could always add drumsticks, which I separate from the thighs if using chicken marylands, as I find that the joints of whole marylands can still appear to be a little 'bloody' even when the chicken is cooked. Never be tempted to serve this as soon as it comes out of the oven – as always, it is much more luscious after resting, and I rely on this time to finish off the cooking.

1 kg free-range chicken thigh
  fillets, skin-on
2 tablespoons rosemary leaves
⅓ cup (80 ml) extra virgin olive oil
sea salt
60 g unsalted butter

2 wedges preserved lemon, rinsed, flesh
  removed and rind thinly sliced
1½ tablespoons lemon thyme leaves
⅓ cup (80 ml) verjuice
roughly chopped flat-leaf parsley, to serve

1 Preheat the oven to 220°C fan-forced (240 °C conventional). Line a baking tray with baking paper and set aside.

2 Place the chicken on a large plate, sprinkle over the rosemary and drizzle with a little of the olive oil, then season the skin with 2 teaspoons salt and set aside for 5 minutes.

3 Melt 30 g of the butter in a large heavy-based non-stick frying pan over medium–high heat and cook for 2–3 minutes until nut-brown, adding a splash of the olive oil when the butter starts to bubble to prevent it from burning. Reduce the heat to medium and add half of the chicken, skin-side down, then cook for 3–4 minutes or just until the skin is light-golden brown. Turn and seal on the other side for 2 minutes. Transfer the chicken to the prepared baking tray, then pour over the pan juices. Repeat with the remaining butter, a little more of the olive oil and remaining chicken.

4 Sprinkle the chicken with the preserved lemon and lemon thyme, then bake for 6–8 minutes or until just cooked through. Remove from the oven and drizzle with the verjuice, then leave to rest for 5–6 minutes.

5 Place the chicken on a serving platter with the resting juices, then sprinkle with parsley and drizzle with the remaining olive oil. Serve. (Any leftover chicken can be stored in airtight container in the fridge for up to 2 days.)

ROASTED ALMOND JELLY
WITH CHERRY COMPOTE

Serves 8

I often made blancmange back in my restaurant days – an old-fashioned dessert if ever there was one. Here, in thinking how lovely it would be for Christmas with cherries, I decided to go one step further and roast some almonds, then infuse them in the buttermilk – and back off on the amount of cream I'd normally use. Taking this extra step so delighted me, and the resulting jelly is really wonderful with summer fruit. I've tried it with stewed mulberries (hard to get without having your own tree), the ripest of apricots (see opposite), and here, with the large, dark cherries that just have a touch of acidity, which I love so much – not least because they speak to me of Christmastime.

200 ml thickened cream
300 g flaked almonds
400 ml buttermilk
30 g caster sugar
140 ml water
2½ × 2 g gold-strength gelatine leaves
2 cups (500 ml) cold water
extra roasted slivered almonds, to serve

CHERRY COMPOTE
600 g cherries
50 g caster sugar
⅓ cup (80 ml) verjuice
⅓ cup (80 ml) water

1 Using hand-held electric beaters, whisk the cream in a bowl until soft peaks form. Set aside.

2 Preheat the oven to 200°C fan-forced (220°C conventional).

3 Place the almonds on a baking tray lined with baking paper and roast for 8–10 minutes or until light golden, checking frequently as they burn easily. Leave to cool completely. Place in a food processor and blitz until finely ground, then transfer to a bowl.

4 Place the buttermilk in a small heavy-based saucepan over low heat and bring just to simmering point. Immediately pour over the ground almonds and leave to infuse for 1 hour. Strain the milk through clean muslin or a Chux cloth, squeezing out all the almond-infused buttermilk. Measure and reserve 100 ml for making the jelly. Discard the almonds.

5 Place the caster sugar and water in a clean small saucepan over low heat, stirring for 1 minute to dissolve the sugar, then heat to warm through. Remove from the heat. Meanwhile, soak the gelatine leaves in a bowl with the cold water to soften, then gently squeeze out any excess water. Immediately add the gelatine to the warm sugar syrup and stir until it has dissolved.

6 Stir the reserved almond-infused buttermilk into the sugar-syrup mixture until well combined, then fold through one-quarter of this into the whipped cream at a time

until all the buttermilk and sugar-syrup mixture are incorporated. Pour into a 2-cup (500 ml)-capacity serving dish and refrigerate for 3–4 hours or until set.

7 Meanwhile, make the compote. Place the cherries, caster sugar, verjuice and water in a large heavy-based saucepan over low heat and stir to dissolve the sugar. Bring to a simmer, then simmer gently for 10 minutes or until the cherries have softened. Remove from the heat and leave to cool. Remove the cherries from the syrup (squash the pips out, if desired, although I leave them in) and set aside. Bring the syrup to a simmer over medium heat, then simmer for 1–2 minutes to reduce a little. Remove the pan from the heat, then return the cherries to the pan and set aside until ready to serve.

8 Serve the jelly with the cherry compote, scattered with extra slivered almonds.

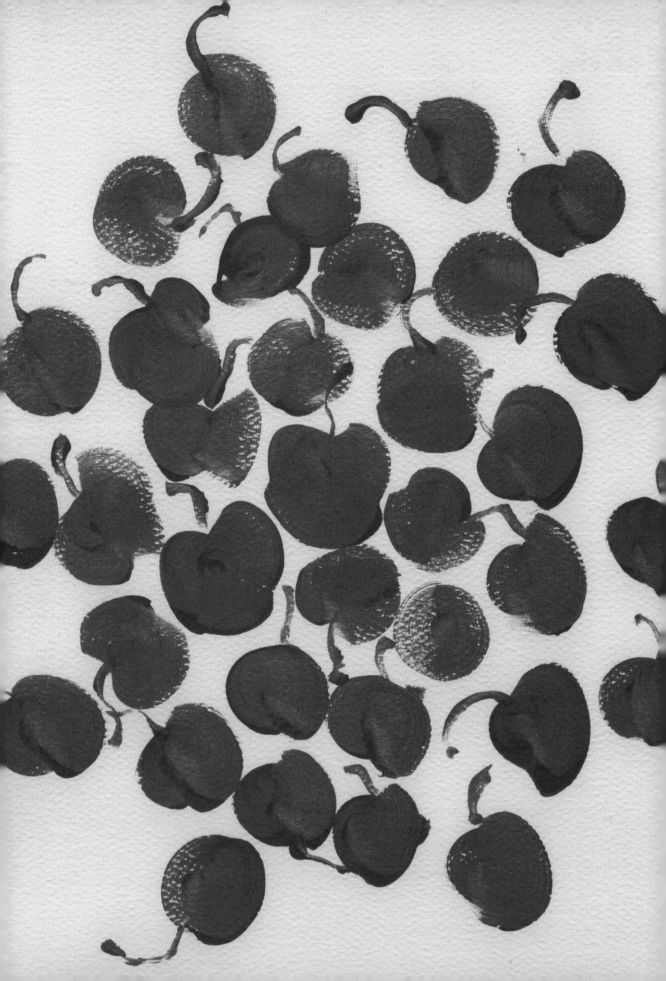

Christmas Day Lunch

I HAVE NEVER LOST THE EXCITEMENT OF CHRISTMAS DAY and all it entails. From my earliest childhood memories, this has nothing to do with extravagant gifts, but rather it's about sharing the day, and the pleasures of a bountiful table, with family. Each year, from when our children were young to the advent of our grandchildren, Zöe, Max, Lilly, Rory and Ben, our delight comes from the children. I have photos from over the years of the same scene in our front room. The pine tree takes centre stage, with its Christmas-y scent pervading, adorned with ornaments of varying levels of sophistication that differ from year to year, depending on which grandchild has helped Colin to decorate. One constant is the silver cardboard and tinsel star at the very top, made by Saskia and Elli when they were little. Bread-dough angels made by an on old friend always find their way onto the tree, as do fairy lights that compete with the tinsel and whatever coloured balls we manage to find that still have their string attached. There is no such thing as 'less is more' when it comes to the tree. Another constant is Colin playing Santa Claus, dating from when Zöe and Max were babies – if truth be told, this bit was never more exciting than when they were really little and just tearing off wrapping paper was enough of a thrill!

The only change I've seen over the years is that, with just the two of us at home now, I no longer need to get up early on Christmas morning. Having completed every possible bit of preparation the day before leaves this as a day to enjoy with family. My morning ritual is to put on my coffee machine and turn on the radio to listen to my much-loved ABC Classic FM, where I can be sure to hear beautiful music. The doors and windows are opened and I turn up the music as loud as Colin will abide. Breakfast will be a little special: perhaps scrambled eggs with the cured ocean trout (see page 145) leftover from Christmas Eve and a jar of salmon roe (or sometimes caviar), as an indulgent treat to gild the lily. The turkey and goose are brought out of the fridge to come to room temperature, and the oven is preheated for roasting. It's then time for phone calls to my brothers, one in Sydney and the other in Queensland, and to Colin's family.

With the poultry safely cooking in a low oven, we drive a few kilometres to visit our friends the Schuberts, where, for the last 35 years we've had a Christmas drink with them and many other locals. It's a wonderful chance to see so many friends, who then go on to spend the rest of the day with their own families. Each couple takes a bottle of Champagne, and Tia Schubert, the wonderful host that she is, has a leg of ham to slice off the bone, pastries hot from the oven and other nibbles to accompany the unaccustomed morning tipple. By now, though, its 11 am, and only an hour before afternoon begins!

It's such a lovely gathering – the trick is not to have so much fun I forget the poultry in the oven and that the family will be arriving at home between 12:30 and 1 pm. We'll be in trouble with the grandchildren if we're late as there are presents to open before lunch is served!

After this, the front room can look like a hurricane has hit, and it always seems to be the grown-ups who pick up the wrapping paper and tidy the room, with the children outside playing, happy to wait for lunch. The turkey and goose will be ready to be removed from the oven and rested, in which time their internal temperature will increase and the pork will have its turn in the already hot oven – time now to cook the yabbies in the courtyard. There is a definite division of duties, with my daughters and grandchildren helping me with the final touches on the food and the boys cleaning up – it may seem sexist, but it's more about the skill of the individuals.

Lunch is then served in the garden and no one minds when the children leave the table to play a game of cricket on the front lawn. Another thing that never changes is that, as soon as everyone has left, I sneak off to bed for a snooze – tired but happy . . .

Christmas Day Lunch

Menu for 8

Salad of yabbies and nectarines ~ 172

Figs with burrata and mint ~ 174

Lobster sashimi with rockmelon and lime ~ 177

Roast goose with marmalade and cumquat stuffing and goose-fat roasted potatoes ~ 180
and/or Roast turkey with prune and orange stuffing and Cumberland sauce ~ 184
and/or Roast pork loin with verjuice and grapes ~ 190

Roasted capsicum with Persian feta and eggplant and parsley salad ~ 192

Salad of paw paw, mango and rocket ~ 195

Poached white peaches with sparkling ruby jelly and clotted cream ~ 198

Christmas pudding with cumquat brandy butter ~ 202

SALAD OF YABBIES AND NECTARINES

Serves 8 as a starter

Including yabbies on our Christmas menu is a long-standing family tradition, dating back to when we first moved to our current home from the Pheasant Farm. Saskia was 12 and Elli 10 at the time and they didn't want to move; the only enticement was the dam at the bottom of the garden – the best yabby dam in the district, before the droughts. We only had a temporary lean-to kitchen for the first two years, and being summer when we moved in, we sat at a table in the garden every evening to enjoy our catch of yabbies. That's how it was that yabbies were the hero of the meal on our first Christmas in the cottage, and have been ever since, even though now the dam is not the yabby beacon it was back then due to so many dry years (the upside is no more poachers!).

We now supplement our catch with yabbies from the farmers' market when we need to, and there have been years when, in desperation, we've ordered yabbies all the way from Western Australia – that's how important they are to us at this time of year. The addition of nectarines comes from the beautiful heritage orchard we now own, so we are lucky to have the first of our own ripe stone fruit ready in time for Christmas Day.

16 large yabbies (about 80 g each)
zest of 1 lemon, removed in wide strips
　　with no bitter white pith
3 large yellow nectarines, cut into halves,
　　stones removed and thinly sliced
1 cos lettuce, leaves separated, washed
　　and dried
1 head red witlof, leaves separated,
　　washed and dried
1 head white witlof, leaves separated,
　　washed and dried

1 large handful purslane or other soft
　　salad leaves
micro-mint or small mint leaves, to serve

VERJUICE VINAIGRETTE
⅓ cup (80 ml) verjuice
⅓ cup (80 ml) extra virgin olive oil
1 teaspoon Dijon mustard
sea salt and freshly ground black pepper

1 Place the yabbies in the freezer for 20 minutes or until they are asleep. Meanwhile, place the lemon zest in a small saucepan and cover with water, then bring to the boil. Simmer for 2 minutes, then drain and set aside to cool.

2 Bring a large saucepan of water to the boil. Add 8 of the yabbies to the pan and cover with a lid to bring the water back to the boil as quickly as possible. Remove the lid as soon as the water returns to the boil to prevent it from overflowing. Boil the yabbies for 3 minutes or until just cooked through; it is important not to crowd the pan so they cook quickly. Scoop out the yabbies and spread them on a platter, then set aside to cool. (I like to remove the yabbies using a wire basket with a handle.) Return the water to the boil, then repeat with the remaining yabbies. Set aside to cool.

3 Meanwhile, to make the vinaigrette, place the verjuice, olive oil, mustard and salt and pepper to taste in a small bowl and whisk to combine.

4 Peel the cooled yabbies and place the flesh in a large bowl. Add the nectarines, leaves, lemon zest and vinaigrette and gently mix to combine. Scatter with mint and serve.

FIGS WITH BURRATA AND MINT

Serves 8 as a starter

Anyone who tastes burrata will love it – that is, if they love fresh, unctuous, creamy cheese. It's really a ball of fresh molten mozzarella, made from cow's or buffalo's milk, that is patted out like pizza dough, then filled with shredded mozzarella mixed with fresh 'real' cream. The external layer of mozzarella is then tied to enclose the filling, much like a 'beggar's purse', while still very hot. I was so excited to be taught how to do this by Pino at La Vera Mozzarella in Adelaide when filming my ABC TV Christmas special that aired in December 2012. You need to balance something so very rich with something slightly acidic. Here I've used the first flush of figs from my garden, picked just in time for Christmas. At other times I've used really ripe tomatoes roasted with extra virgin olive oil and basil, or ripe peaches, also with basil and a vino cotto vinaigrette.

6 small balls fresh burrata (if not available, use fior di latte)
6 figs, sliced crossways
1½ tablespoons vino cotto

⅓ cup (80 ml) extra virgin olive oil
sea salt and freshly ground black pepper
micro-mint or thinly sliced mint, to serve

1 Place the burrata in the centre of one or two large serving plates or dishes in a single layer. Arrange the fig slices around, then drizzle with vino cotto. Gently pierce the centre of each burrata and pull aside a little to show the creamy centre. Drizzle the burrata and figs with olive oil and sprinkle the burrata with salt and the figs with pepper, then scatter with mint and serve.

LOBSTER SASHIMI
WITH ROCKMELON AND LIME

Serves 8 as a starter

I know that lobster will always be an expensive addition to the table, unless you have your own lobster pot! Recently, my daughter Saskia organised live lobsters through friends as my Christmas present. For me, when it comes to enjoying lobster, I choose sashimi every time. So I did a deal with my family to prepare half of the lobster as I've done here with the ripest rockmelon and lime (lemon will work just as well), and the rest poached in a salad with potatoes and tarragon mayonnaise (see page 220). The South Australian company Ferguson's Lobsters actually supply cryovaced prepared frozen sashimi, which makes the whole job easier. However, this product is only available in February, when they have large lobsters to work with. Simplicity is the absolute essence of this dish, so if you don't have fresh lobster and ripe rockmelon, leave this one out.

1 ripe rockmelon (cantaloupe), seeded,
   peeled and cut into 2 cm dice
¼ cup (60 ml) extra virgin olive oil
3 limes, 2 cut in half and very thinly sliced
   and 1 for squeezing

400 g sashimi lobster, chilled
handful mint, sliced
sea salt and freshly ground black pepper

1 Toss the rockmelon with 2 tablespoons of the olive oil and the lime juice. Place on a platter, then top with the lime slices.

2 Thinly slice the lobster with a sharp flexible knife, then place in a mound on top of the rockmelon and lime. Drizzle with the remaining olive oil, then scatter with mint, season with salt and pepper and serve.

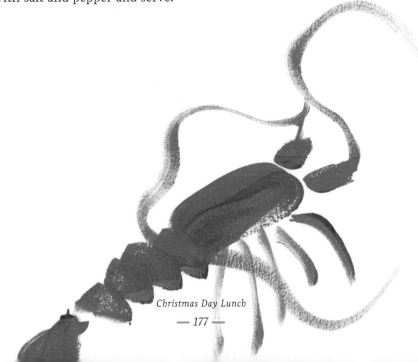

Roast goose
with marmalade
and cumquat
stuffing

ROAST GOOSE WITH MARMALADE AND CUMQUAT STUFFING AND GOOSE-FAT ROASTED POTATOES

Serves 8–10 as part of a buffet

This recipe goes back to my childhood days, when Mum and Dad would have a roast goose on the table at Christmastime. Not that I imagine it was easy to get hold of, but my Uncle Leo had a farm on the outskirts of Sydney and raised a few geese. Colin and I have grown our own geese since the late 1970s, although not in commercial quantities, and our daughter Saskia now has them grown for her, so we've always had a stash for special occasions and to share with the occasional foodie friend. Over the years we've learnt that if we try to keep a goose until Christmas it will be eight months past its best eating time, and an old goose is a tough goose. Our compromise is to despatch a goose at the right age, then freeze it for Christmas – luckily they freeze well due to their abundance of fat. Marmalade and cumquats cut through this incredible richness, but don't waste the fat – use it to roast the potatoes.

1 × 2.5 kg goose
¾ cup (255 g) Seville marmalade
3 tablespoons rosemary leaves, plus
   extra stems, to serve (optional)
1 tablespoon extra virgin olive oil
sea salt
1 teaspoon plain flour
¼ cup (60 ml) verjuice
Maggie Beer Dried Mustard Apricots
   (available from maggiebeer.com.au)
   drained, (reserve the syrup to brush over
   any poultry before cooking), to serve

CUMQUAT STUFFING
30 g sliced dehydrated cumquats
   (available from tolleysnurseries.com.au)
¼ cup (60 ml) warm water

½ cup (125 ml) extra virgin olive oil
2 onions, roughly chopped
4 cloves garlic, chopped
2 tablespoons rosemary, finely chopped
100 g sliced belly bacon
large handful flat-leaf parsley,
   roughly chopped
2 tablespoons thyme, chopped
3 cups (210 g) coarse fresh
   white breadcrumbs
sea salt and freshly ground black pepper

GOOSE-FAT ROASTED POTATOES
1 kg Jersey Gold or other waxy potatoes,
   cut into quarters
sea salt
2 tablespoons plain flour

1 To make the stuffing, soak the cumquats in a bowl with the warm water for 10 minutes. Heat ¼ cup (60 ml) of the olive oil in a large heavy-based non-stick frying pan over medium heat. Cook the onion, stirring occasionally, for 15 minutes or until golden brown. Add the garlic and rosemary and cook for 3–4 minutes. Drain the cumquats and set aside, reserving the liquid. Add the liquid to the pan, stirring to deglaze. Simmer for 1 minute or until the liquid has reduced and become syrupy. Remove from the heat.

2 Place another non-stick frying pan over high heat, then dry-cook the belly bacon for 5 minutes on each side or until crisp. Drain on paper towel until cool enough to handle, then cut off and discard the rind and roughly chop the remainder into 1 cm pieces.

3 Preheat the oven to 120°C fan-forced (140°C conventional).

4 Place the cumquats, parsley, thyme, breadcrumbs and remaining olive oil in a bowl, then mix together well. Add the warm onion mixture and bacon, then season to taste with salt and pepper and mix to combine. Fill the goose cavity with the stuffing mixture.

5 Mix together the marmalade, rosemary, olive oil and 2 teaspoons salt and massage all over the goose. Tuck the wings behind. Place the flour in a large oven bag and shake to distribute the flour throughout the bag. Slide the goose into the oven bag to coat it with flour. Tie the end of the bag well with kitchen string and slip it into another oven bag, then seal this too. Place the goose in a baking dish or roasting pan.

6 Roast the goose for 2 hours 20 minutes (this time is for a 2.5 kg goose – you will need to adjust the time depending on the weight and age of the goose you buy). To test whether your goose is cooked, look through the oven bag and check that the meat has come away from the leg bones; the breastbone will have just started to protrude and the goose will feel 'done', that is, just 'giving', to the touch.

7 Remove the goose from the oven. Cut a corner off the oven bag, then carefully pour all the juices and fat through a fine-mesh sieve into the tallest, thinnest jug you have; using a jug with the smallest surface area will accelerate the setting of the fat. Place the jug in the fridge to chill so that the fat will separate from the juice.

8 If the goose is not golden brown, remove it from the oven bag and place it on a baking tray, breast-side up. Increase the oven temperature to 180°C fan-forced (200°C conventional), then return the goose to the oven for 10 minutes or until golden all over. Immediately pour the verjuice over.

9 Place the hot goose, breast-side down, in the dish/pan. Leave to rest for up to 1 hour with the oven bag or a sheet of foil loosely covering it; it will retain its heat.

10 Once the fat has set, scoop it from the jug and set aside for roasting the potatoes. (If the fat has not set, use a small ladle to scoop off the top layer of fat, then transfer it to a roasting pan – you should have at least 1 cup [250 ml]). Place the remaining cooking juices in a small saucepan over medium heat, then simmer for 10 minutes or until reduced by half. Strain and keep warm until ready to serve.

11 Meanwhile, to roast the potatoes, place them in a saucepan, then cover with cold water. Season with salt and bring to the boil, then simmer until just tender. Drain well and leave to dry out for at least 10 minutes to allow excess moisture to evaporate. Lightly dust the potatoes all over with the flour just before roasting.

12 Preheat the oven to 220°C fan-forced (240°C conventional). Place the roasting pan with the reserved goose fat in the oven for 5 minutes or until sizzling, then add the potatoes in a single layer. Roast the potatoes for 10 minutes, then turn over and roast for a further 10 minutes or until golden and crisp. Sprinkle with a little salt.

13 Serve the goose, stuffing, roasted potatoes and mustard apricots with the warm pan juices offered alongside, garnished with extra rosemary stems, if desired.

Roast turkey, with prune and orange Stuffing and Cumberland Sauce

ROAST TURKEY WITH PRUNE AND ORANGE STUFFING AND CUMBERLAND SAUCE

Serves 12–16 as part of a buffet

I'd never bothered with turkey, always feeling that it was a dry bird. Because goose was our first choice for Christmas, I'd never actually cooked a turkey until Colin started breeding them for the Christmas market. Of course, these were free-ranged and fed a corn diet, so I changed my mind completely. For the stuffing, I used the Seville oranges in verjuice syrup we make for the Farmshop; its wonderful bittersweet edge, combined with the prunes and rosemary, are a great match for turkey. You could use marmalade mixed with grated orange zest instead – or the cumquat stuffing on page 180. The Cumberland sauce is a good substitute for making gravy. I first came across this recipe in the *Game Conservancy Cookbook*, when Colin and I visited the United Kingdom for his Churchill Fellowship to study game-bird breeding – the start of this whole journey of ours. I've tickled it a bit by adding horseradish, and it's great served either hot or cold.

1 × 6.6 kg free-range corn-fed turkey
1 teaspoon plain flour

PRUNE AND ORANGE STUFFING
⅔ cup (160 ml) extra virgin olive oil
2 large onions, roughly chopped
2 tablespoons finely chopped
  flat-leaf parsley
1 tablespoon finely chopped rosemary
3 tablespoons finely chopped lemon thyme
4 cups (280 g) loosely packed coarse fresh
  white breadcrumbs
200 g pitted prunes, cut in half
1 × 360 g jar Maggie Beer Seville Oranges
  in Spiced Verjuice Syrup (available from
  maggiebeer.com.au), finely chopped
sea salt and freshly ground black pepper

CUMBERLAND SAUCE
finely grated zest of 2 oranges,
  plus 100 ml juice
finely grated zest of 2 lemons,
  plus ⅓ cup (80 ml) juice
⅓ cup (140 g) redcurrant jelly
1 heaped teaspoon Dijon mustard
½ teaspoon ground ginger
½ cup (125 ml) port
½ cup (115 g) horseradish cream (available
  in jars from specialty food stores)

1 To make the Cumberland sauce, place the orange and lemon zest and juice, redcurrant jelly, mustard, ginger and port in a saucepan. Bring to a simmer over medium–high heat, stirring to combine, then cook for 20 minutes or until it thickens a little. Leave to cool completely, then stir in the horseradish cream. Cover with plastic film and refrigerate until needed. Store in a sterilised jar in the fridge for up to 1 week. (Makes about 1¼ cups [310 ml].)

2 Preheat the oven to 140°C fan-forced (160°C conventional). »

3 To make the stuffing, heat the olive oil in a heavy-based non-stick frying pan over medium heat. Add the onion and cook for 20 minutes or until dark golden and slightly browned around the edges. Set aside. Combine the parsley, rosemary, thyme, breadcrumbs, prunes, orange and onion in a bowl, then season with 3 teaspoons salt and pepper to taste. Fill the turkey cavity with the stuffing mixture. Fold the wings under the body and then truss it well with kitchen string.

4 Place the flour in an extra-large oven bag and shake to distribute the flour throughout the bag. Slide the turkey into the bag to coat it with flour. Tie the end of the bag well with kitchen string and slip it into another oven bag, then seal this too. Place the turkey in a baking dish or roasting pan, then roast for 2½ hours or until golden and cooked through.

5 Remove the turkey from the oven. Cut a corner off the oven bag, then carefully pour all the juices and fat into the tallest, thinnest jug you have (so you have the smallest surface area) to accelerate the fat setting. Place the jug in the fridge to chill so that the fat will separate from the juice. Place the piping-hot turkey, breast-side down, in the dish/pan. Leave the turkey to rest for up to 1 hour with the torn oven bag or a sheet of foil loosely covering it; it will retain its heat in this time.

6 If the turkey is not golden brown, remove it from the oven bag and place it on a baking tray, breast-side up. Increase the oven temperature to 180°C fan-forced (200°C conventional), then return the turkey to the oven for 10 minutes or until golden all over.

7 Once the fat has set, scoop it from the jug and discard. Place the juices in a small saucepan, then bring to the boil over high heat and simmer for 10 minutes or until reduced by half. Strain and keep warm until ready to serve.

8 Serve the turkey and stuffing with the pan juices and Cumberland sauce.

ROAST PORK LOIN WITH VERJUICE AND GRAPES

Serves 8 as part of a banquet

I've often written that I wasn't interested in eating pork, with the exception of the Christmas ham, until our first real trip to Italy, when I experienced an epiphany upon eating pork spiedini. Grilled on a charcoal barbecue, I couldn't believe how amazing they tasted – so foreign from any pork I'd eaten before. Upon returning home, I found that Colin and Joy Lienert of Sheoak Log have bred free-range Berkshire pigs on grains they grow themselves for over 60 years, here on the edge of the Barossa. Fortunately, they never went along with the trend of breeding fat out of their pigs (and the fat of Berkshire pork is beautifully sweet) and rejected intensive growing. For me, the lovely part of this story is that, in 2004, Saskia started using these pigs for her Black Pig brand of charcuterie and fresh produce. I've done a total turnaround and now love pork. If you can't find Berkshire pork try the other heritage breeds passionate farmers are producing – you'll be amazed by the difference to regular pork. You need to prepare the pork, then refrigerate it overnight to achieve the best crackling.

1 × 2 kg free-range pork loin (I use
   Berkshire pork), skin-on, scored
   (ask your butcher to do this)
1 litre boiling water
½ cup (125 g) sea salt
6 tablespoons fennel seeds

finely grated zest of 2 lemons
6 bay leaves
2 tablespoons verjuice
1 tablespoon French tarragon leaves
350 g seedless green grapes, cut in half

1 Place the pork, skin-side up, on a wire rack over the sink and pour the boiling water over to open up the cuts in the skin. Rub the salt, fennel seeds and zest into the skin and crush the bay leaves on top. Transfer the pork to a wire rack over a baking tray, then refrigerate overnight.

2 Remove the pork from the fridge and leave to come to room temperature for 30–60 minutes. Scrape off the excess salt mixture with a knife.

3 Preheat the oven to its highest setting – generally 240°C or 250°C (fan-forced and conventional).

4 Place the pork, skin-side up, in a roasting pan and roast for 30 minutes for just pink inside; the internal temperature should register 62°C on a meat thermometer, resulting in just-cooked, succulent meat. Immediately pour off the fat from the pan, then add the tarragon to the pan juices and set aside. Drizzle the flesh-sides of the pork with the verjuice (do not drizzle the crackling as it will soften), then leave to rest in a warm spot for 15 minutes. (The temperature should be retested after 5 minutes, and it should have increased to 69°C or 70°C.) Spoon off any excess fat from the juices.

5 Place the pork, skin-side down, on a chopping board (this makes it easier to cut through the crackling), then cut into thin slices, using the scored lines as your guide. Serve the pork with the pan juices, garnished with the grapes.

ROASTED CAPSICUM WITH PERSIAN FETA AND EGGPLANT AND PARSLEY SALAD

Serves 4 as a main

There has to be a vegetable dish somewhere to balance out the richness of the goose, turkey and pork – and I wanted to create something special for my vegetarian granddaughter. As my whole premise on Christmas Day is to prepare as much as possible the day before, this dish fits the bill. You can roast the capsicums and prepare the filling in advance, then assemble the dish on the day. As there is no chance of having capsicums ready in my garden, I chose the richest red medium-sized capsicums I could find at the farmers' market, so that they'd sit up well and be easy to fill. The parsley salad alongside has had many incarnations, and each time it never fails to surprise me with how good it is, especially (you won't be surprised to hear!) when the parsley comes from my own garden. This part can only be made at the last minute – but then, I love having something still to be done, whether I am feeding family or friends.

4 large red capsicums (peppers)
½ cup (125 ml) extra virgin olive oil
2 small eggplants (aubergines),
  (about 280 g each), cut into 2 cm pieces
3 slices sourdough, crusts removed, torn
  (to yield about 90 g torn bread)
180 g Persian feta, well drained
finely grated zest of 1 lemon
sea salt and freshly ground black pepper

PARSLEY SALAD
100 ml extra virgin olive oil
2 tablespoons large salted capers, rinsed
  and drained
½ red onion, finely chopped
1 large handful flat-leaf parsley leaves
12 kalamata olives, pitted
zest of 1 lemon, removed in long, thin strips
1 tablespoon lemon juice
1 teaspoon pomegranate molasses

1 Place the capsicums directly over a gas or barbecue burner, then cook on each side for 4 minutes or until the skin has blackened and blistered. Immediately place in a plastic bag and seal, then leave to sweat for 10 minutes to make it easier to remove the skins. Remove the warm capsicums from the bag, then peel, taking care not to tear or break the flesh. Cut the tops off and remove the seeds. Set aside.

2 Preheat the oven to 180°C fan-forced (200°C conventional). Line a baking tray with baking paper.

3 Heat ¼ cup (60 ml) of the olive oil a large heavy-based non-stick frying pan over high heat. Add the eggplant and cook for 5–6 minutes or until dark-golden brown on all sides, stirring every 20–30 seconds so that it doesn't burn. Drain the eggplant on paper towel. Add the remaining olive oil to the pan. Once the oil is hot, add the bread and cook for 2–3 minutes, turning until golden brown on both sides. Drain on paper towel.

4 Leave the eggplant and bread to cool for 5 minutes, then transfer to a mixing bowl. Add the feta and lemon zest, then season to taste with salt and pepper and mix together well.

5 Divide the stuffing evenly among the capsicums. Place the capsicums on the prepared tray, then roast for 6–8 minutes to warm through.

6 Meanwhile, make the salad. Heat 2 tablespoons of the olive oil in a small frying pan over high heat. Add the capers and fry for 20 seconds, then drain on paper towel. Transfer the capers to a bowl, then add the onion, parsley, olives and lemon zest and gently toss together. Set aside. Place the remaining olive oil, lemon juice and pomegranate molasses in a bowl and whisk together.

7 Just before serving, drizzle the salad with the dressing and gently mix to coat. Divide the capsicums and salad among serving plates, then serve.

SALAD OF PAW PAW, MANGO AND ROCKET

Serves 6–8 as an accompaniment

A Christmas salad if ever there was one – all these flavours are meant to be together. I try to get a tray of Bowen mangoes, my favourites, from Queensland every summer – somehow even the scent of them says Christmas to me. It's worth seeking out a small red paw paw from a flavour point of view, and buying your avocados in advance so they ripen on the kitchen bench over the days before you use them. So often I find when you need an avocado you can only find either rock-hard ones or squeezed and bruised ripe ones that are black inside.

2 large avocados
2 tablespoons verjuice
1 red paw paw, seeded, peeled and
   cut into 2 cm pieces
3 mangoes, cut into long, thin slices

2 large handfuls rocket
finely grated zest of 2 limes
2 tablespoons lime juice
¼ cup (60 ml) extra virgin olive oil
sea salt and freshly ground black pepper

1 Peel and seed the avocados, then drizzle with the verjuice to prevent them from discolouring. Cut into bite-sized pieces, then place in a bowl. Add the paw paw, mango and rocket.

2 Place the lime zest and juice in a small bowl, then whisk in the olive oil and season to taste with salt and pepper.

3 Just before serving, dress the salad with the lime dressing. Serve at once.

poached white peaches
with sparkling ruby
jelly and clotted
cream

POACHED WHITE PEACHES WITH SPARKLING RUBY JELLY AND CLOTTED CREAM

Serves 8

A ripe white peach picked and eaten straight from a tree on the edge of the garden of our first farmhouse started my whole food journey in the Barossa. Saskia was only six weeks old and we'd moved in just two weeks before Christmas. We sold this house, with its untended orchard, three years later to build what is now the Farmshop across the river. I still vividly remember falling in love with this fruit then and there. When you poach white peaches they transform into a beautiful blush-pink, forming a magical combination with the jelly and richly decadent clotted cream. You will need to make the clotted cream the day before you wish to serve this.

200 g caster sugar
400 ml water
1 × 750 ml bottle Sparkling Ruby Cabernet
  (available from maggiebeer.com.au)
2 vanilla pods, split and seeds scraped
¼ cup (60 ml) brandy
8 ripe white peaches

SPARKLING RUBY JELLY
3 cups (750 ml) syrup from poaching
  the peaches
8 × 2 g gold-strength gelatine leaves
2 cups (500 ml) cold water

CLOTTED CREAM
300 ml thickened cream
½ teaspoon caster sugar

1 To make the clotted cream, place the cream and caster sugar in a small heavy-based saucepan over low–medium heat, then bring to a gentle simmer. Reduce the heat to as low as possible (use a simmer mat if necessary), then simmer for 20 minutes. Remove from the heat. Transfer to a glass bowl, then cover the surface closely with plastic film and refrigerate overnight. In this time the cream will thicken to the texture of double cream and be absolutely luscious.

2 Place the caster sugar and water in a small saucepan over medium heat, stirring until the sugar has dissolved. Bring to the boil, then immediately remove from the heat. Pour the sugar syrup into a wide, deep, heavy-based frying pan, then add the wine and vanilla pods and seeds and bring to the boil over high heat. Add the brandy and burn off the alcohol by carefully placing a lit match close to the surface. Boil the syrup over high heat for 15 minutes or until it has reduced to 900 ml. Remove from the heat and remove the vanilla pods.

3 Place the peaches in a clean saucepan that holds them snugly in one layer. Pour the reduced syrup over the peaches, then cover them with a heatproof saucer to weight them down so they are covered in syrup. Cook the peaches over low heat for 5 minutes. Carefully remove the peaches and transfer to a plate, reserving the poaching syrup. Leave the peaches to cool for 10 minutes or until cool enough to handle, then carefully

peel off the skins. Transfer to a bowl, cover with plastic film and set aside at room temperature until required.

4 Meanwhile, make the jelly. Strain the warm poaching syrup and measure 3 cups (750 ml). Soften the gelatine leaves in a bowl with the cold water for 5 minutes and squeeze out any excess water. Add the softened gelatine to the warm poaching liquid and whisk together well until the gelatine has dissolved. Pour into an 800 ml-capacity glass bowl and refrigerate for 3 hours or until set.

5 Just before serving, turn the jelly out onto a serving plate, if you like. To do this, dip the base of the bowl into a bowl of hot water for 20–30 seconds, then gently invert the bowl of jelly over the serving plate. Alternatively, serve the jelly straight from the bowl. Place the poached peaches in a serving bowl, then serve at the centre of the table with the jelly and clotted cream offered separately.

Christmas pudding
with cumquat
brandy butter

CHRISTMAS PUDDING WITH CUMQUAT BRANDY BUTTER

Serves 20

Our family never manages to eat the Christmas pudding on Christmas Day. What tends to happen is that it's covered well and put back into the fridge. In the evenings that follow, it is taken out a slice at a time and warmed a little, to enjoy with a cup of tea after dinner. Traditionally, Christmas pudding is made in advance to allow time for it to mature – I make ours in October. The pudding will keep for a long time, as will the brandy butter – that is, if you don't eat it by the spoonful when you pass the fridge like I do, butter fiend that I am. It would be much better for me if I didn't make the brandy butter at all, but then it wouldn't be Christmas!

365 g dehydrated cumquats (available from tolleysnurseries.com.au), or any mixed peel if not available
225 g currants
225 g seedless raisins
225 g sultanas
1 cup (250 ml) cumquat brandy or regular brandy
115 g plain flour, plus extra for dusting
good pinch of ground cinnamon
good pinch of freshly grated nutmeg
good pinch of ground ginger
good pinch of ground mace

sea salt
225 g chilled unsalted butter
225 g fresh breadcrumbs
finely grated zest of 2 lemons
2 granny smith apples, peeled and grated
75 g flaked almonds
3 free-range eggs

CUMQUAT BRANDY BUTTER
175 g icing sugar
175 g unsalted butter, softened
½ cup (125 ml) cumquat brandy or regular brandy

1 Combine the cumquats, currants, raisins, sultanas and brandy in a large non-reactive bowl and mix thoroughly. Cover with plastic film and leave at room temperature for 24 hours, stirring several times.

2 Sift the flour, cinnamon, nutmeg, ginger, mace and 1 teaspoon salt into a large bowl, then coarsely grate in the butter. Stir in the breadcrumbs and add the lemon zest, apple, almonds and fruit mixture. Whisk the eggs until light and frothy and stir through the pudding mixture until well combined.

3 For one large pudding, dust a 60 cm square of calico with a little extra flour, then spoon the pudding mixture into the middle. Gather up the cloth and tie it securely with kitchen string at the top to enclose the pudding. Steam the pudding in a large double steamer over boiling water or boil in a large saucepan for 6 hours, replenishing the water every 30 minutes or as necessary. (To make two puddings, divide the mixture in half and wrap each in a 40 cm square of dusted calico, then steam or boil as above in separate pans for 4 hours.)

4 Suspend the boiled pudding in a cool, airy place to mature before serving. (Christmas puddings certainly mature with standing, but the main issues are having the right

balance of flavours in the first place and ensuring a long cooking time. Puddings can become mouldy in humid weather or if several are hung too close together, so if you don't have time to mature your pudding, or the weather is against you, don't fret; as long as the flavour balance is fine, it will still be fabulous.)

5 Make the cumquat brandy butter on Christmas morning (it can be made the day before, but it needs to be wrapped really well to avoid it becoming tainted in the refrigerator). Cream the icing sugar and butter in an electric mixer until white, thick and fluffy and the sugar has dissolved; this takes some time, so be patient. Slowly beat in the brandy, a teaspoonful at a time, tasting as you go. Cover with plastic film and refrigerate until required.

6 To serve, steam the pudding in its cloth in the top of a steamer or double saucepan over simmering water for 1 hour or until heated through, checking and topping up the water if necessary. (Having said all that, you can also warm the pudding in a microwave on defrost setting, as long as it is well covered.) Meanwhile, let the brandy butter stand at room temperature for 20 minutes, then transfer to 2 serving bowls.

7 Serve the pudding with the brandy butter.

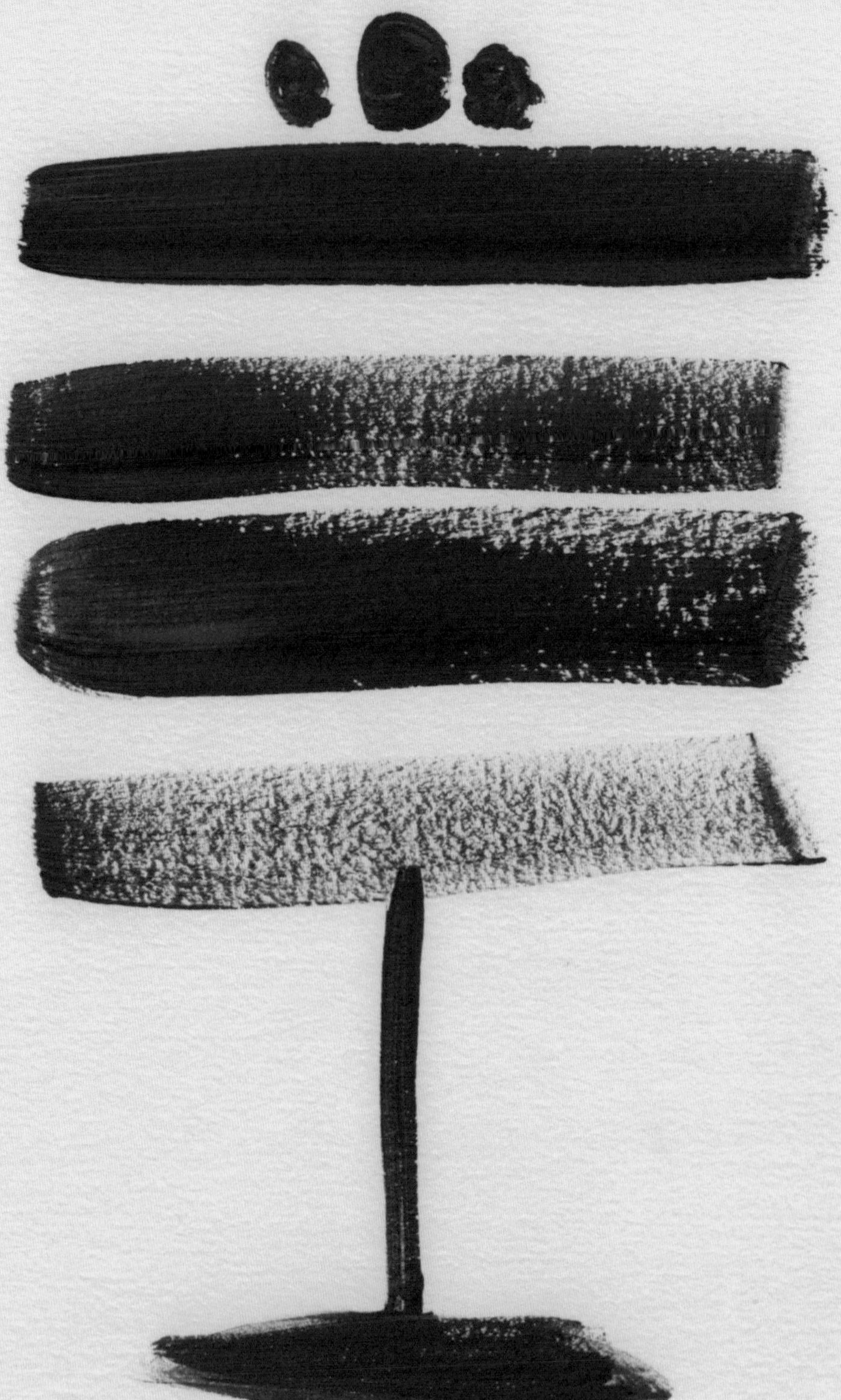

Boxing Day Leftovers

I AM ALWAYS AMAZED THAT ANYONE CAN POSSIBLY BE hungry after the ritual of spending most of Christmas Day eating. However, the torpor of the day after, and the fact that perhaps our stomachs have expanded, overtakes and inevitably we are hungry. Yet, whatever food we eat, it has to be easy.

In all honesty I'll say that Boxing Day is about the least structured day of the year for meals in our house. It's all about what you have leftover and what you can do with it easily when you finally feel hungry. The recipes that follow needn't be restricted to Boxing Day – they are just some of my ideas for making the most of the Christmas bounty. I'm proud of using leftovers, having a real horror of wasting food. I've learnt from my great friend Stephanie Alexander that, not only is there an art to doing leftovers well, there is a fair bit of competition in making dishes out of them that are every bit as tasty as dishes made from scratch.

I know that simple slices of ham with a ripe tomato salad would do, but here I wanted to show that there are other ways not to waste that beautiful, traditionally smoked ham. Pan-frying thick slices of it with green tomatoes as I've done on page 212 gives the ham a special edge, and I'd do the same to serve alongside fried eggs for breakfast. And whilst the ham and cherry jellies on page 219 require you feeling up to a little cooking, warming verjuice and dissolving gelatine falls into the realm of not bothering much for a great outcome, as long as you keep an eye on the timing. That is, make the jellies first thing so they set before you are hungry.

I've included the toasties for two reasons: first, I love them as they are reminiscent of my childhood; second (and equally as important), they can easily be made by the non-cook in the house.

Although the turkey salad on page 216 and lobster salad on pages 220–1 require a bit more effort, such as making mayonnaise, boiling a few potatoes and frying some stale bread, it's not that onerous when you consider you end up with beautiful dishes that could never be thought of as mere leftovers.

Funnily enough, I've included three desserts, which is very unusual for me – but if ever there's a time for such indulgence, surely it's Boxing Day. Given that we always have ice cream in the freezer, it's only one small step further to have frozen (or bought) brioche to warm in the oven. The combination of warm brioche and cold ice cream (or gelato, if you're being traditional) is just brilliant. Both the trifle and pavlova can be pulled together quickly with some advance planning, with the components made ahead of time and assembled at the last moment. Then again, with planning, you could make the trifle a couple of days before, then keep it well covered in the fridge, so you can luxuriate in it on this 'slow' day.

Pan-fried green
tomatoes and
ham

PAN-FRIED GREEN TOMATOES AND HAM

Serves 1

Who hasn't seen that great film starring Jessica Tandy, *Fried Green Tomatoes at the Whistlestop Café*? Until watching this, I had only made chutney, relish or a fabulous sauce for pasta from the unripe end-of-season tomatoes, but frying green tomatoes in lots of butter really works for me. If you grow your own tomatoes you don't have to wait till the end of the season to enjoy this treat, as tomato bushes inevitably have some green ones already fruiting in December. Using leftovers well is the sign of a good cook. However, I must admit it's possible to tire of slice after slice of leftover ham, so pan-frying gives it a totally different character.

40 g unsalted butter
2 slices leftover ham (see page 112),
   sliced off the bone
2 small green tomatoes, cut into wedges

sea salt and freshly ground black pepper
2 teaspoons vino cotto
roughly chopped flat-leaf parsley, to serve

1 Heat 20 g of the butter in a small heavy-based frying pan over medium heat until melted and sizzling. Add the ham and seal for just a minute on each side so as not to overcook it (remember, it is already cooked).

2 Heat the remaining butter in another small heavy-based frying pan over medium heat until melted and sizzling. Toss the tomato into the pan and season with salt and pepper, then cook for 3–4 minutes or until burnished. Add the vino cotto to the pan, stirring to deglaze. Scatter with flat-leaf parsley.

3 Serve the ham and tomatoes at once.

TOASTIES TWO WAYS: HAM AND GRUYERE AND GOOSE AND SOUR CHERRY JAM

Serves 1

The toastie iron I have is pretty battered. It comes from my childhood when we'd sometimes just have an egg toastie for Sunday supper. I have such fond memories of this that every now and then I remember to make one. When better to pull out the toastie iron than on Boxing Day evening when you have a fridge full of leftovers to contend with. Just make sure you added a wonderful gruyere such as Heidi to your pre-Christmas shopping list in anticipation of making these. Although we have a Morello cherry tree that is ready to pick at this time of year, I must confess that I always make sour cherry jam from tinned or bottled sour cherries so I can prepare it well before the Christmas rush. Then, when I have time to pick the cherries in January, I pickle them whole. Fortunately the birds won't touch the tree – they obviously have a more delicate palate and the sourness doesn't suit!

For each toastie you will need:

40 g unsalted butter
2 thick slices white bread

VERSION 1: HAM AND GRUYERE

50 g leftover ham (see page 112), sliced off the bone
30 g thinly sliced Heidi gruyere

1 Butter each piece of bread generously with 20 g of the butter. Place buttered-side down on a chopping board, then top with the ham and cheese. Top with the other slice of bread, buttered-side up. Cut the crusts off flush with the edge of the toastie iron, then toast in the toastie iron over medium heat for 3 minutes on each side or until golden (or use a sandwich press). Serve hot.

VERSION 2: GOOSE AND SOUR CHERRY JAM

50 g leftover sliced goose (see page 180)
2 teaspoons sour cherry jam

1 Butter each piece of bread generously with 20 g of the butter. Place buttered-side down on a chopping board, then top with the goose and jam. Top with the other slice of bread, buttered-side up. Cut the crusts off flush with the edge of the toastie iron, then toast in the toastie iron over medium heat for 3 minutes on each side or until golden (or use a sandwich press). Serve hot.

Toasties two ways:

ham and gruyere and goose and sour cherry jam.

TURKEY SALAD WITH FIGS, BREAD AND WALNUTS

Serves 4

This salad is so good that I'd make it again in autumn, when the second flush of figs appears, going so far as to buy a portion of turkey from a well-brought up bird especially to enjoy this again (or just use a good-quality chook). Although bread salad is very Italian, I first tried it at Zuni Café in San Francisco, when it had to be ordered as a dish for two, and a whole roast chook was brought to the table. Bread salad has so many possibilities – just be sure that all-important final flourish of extra virgin olive oil comes from a good-quality bottle. And remember my notes about walnuts on page 140 . . .

½ cup (50 g) walnuts
¼ cup (60 ml) extra virgin
   olive oil, plus extra for drizzling
2 cups (140 g) torn bread, with
   crusts removed
350 g leftover turkey (see page 184),
   cut into bite-sized pieces
4 ripe figs, cut into quarters
¼ cup (40 g) kalamata olives, pitted

3 heads witlof, bases trimmed, leaves
   separated, washed and dried
2 large handfuls radicchio, washed,
   dried and torn
1 handful rocket, torn

VINAIGRETTE
2 tablespoons red wine vinegar
¼ cup (60 ml) extra virgin olive oil

1 Preheat the oven to 200°C fan-forced (220°C conventional).

2 Place the walnuts on a baking tray and roast for 5 minutes or until golden, checking them frequently to make sure they don't burn. Immediately wrap in a clean tea towel and rub to remove the skins. Shake the walnuts in a sieve to get rid of the skins, then set aside to cool.

3 To make the vinaigrette, mix the vinegar and olive oil in a large shallow dish or bowl.

4 Heat the olive oil in a heavy-based frying pan over medium–high heat, then add the bread and toss for 1–2 minutes or until golden all over. Drain on paper towel, then immediately add to the dish of vinaigrette. Add the turkey, figs, olives and walnuts and toss together.

5 In a separate bowl, toss the witlof, radicchio and rocket. Transfer to a serving dish, then top with the turkey and bread mixture, drizzle with olive oil and serve.

HAM, CHERRY AND PARSLEY VERJUICE JELLIES

Makes 6

Anyone who has seen my website, maggiebeer.com.au, or *Maggie's Verjuice Cookbook* will know how much I love setting savoury ingredients in a verjuice jelly. Here I've taken the French idea for *jambon persillade*, a flavourful ham and parsley jelly, a step further by making my jelly with verjuice. I'm proud to say this adds a piquancy that takes this provincial dish to a whole new level. I've included cherries as I always have large bowls of them on the kitchen table alongside the mangoes at this time of year, as their colour and flavour mean Christmas to me. So much so that a ready supply of cherries, as well as stollen from our neighbour's bakery, are just what my Farmshop and Export Kitchen team need to get through the hectic weeks of filling our Christmas orders.

1½ cups (375 ml) verjuice
2 teaspoon caster sugar
1 sprig French tarragon,
    plus 6 small sprigs extra
4 × 2 g gold-strength gelatine leaves
2 cups (500 ml) cold water
12 large cherries, pitted and cut in half

240 g leftover ham (see page 112),
    sliced off the bone and cut into
    1.5 cm cubes
2 tablespoons flat-leaf parsley,
    finely chopped
extra virgin olive oil, for drizzling
sea salt

1 Place the verjuice and caster sugar in a small stainless-steel saucepan over low–medium heat, then bring just to a simmer, being careful not to let it boil or the verjuice will become cloudy. Remove from the heat, then add the tarragon.

2 Soak the gelatine leaves in a bowl with the cold water for 5 minutes or until softened. Remove the gelatine and squeeze out any excess liquid. Add to the warm verjuice mixture and stir until the gelatine has dissolved, then set aside to infuse for 10 minutes. Remove the tarragon and leave the verjuice mixture to cool completely.

3 Line six ½ cup (125 ml)-capacity moulds with plastic film. Place a cherry half and a small tarragon sprig in the base of each mould, then add 4 or 5 pieces of ham. Sprinkle with parsley, then add a few cherries and repeat until all the ham, parsley and cherries are used.

4 Divide the verjuice mixture evenly among the moulds, making sure that the ham and cherries are covered so that the set jellies can sit flat when they are turned out. Refrigerate the jellies for 3 hours or until set.

5 To serve, dip each mould into a bowl of hot water for 20–30 seconds, then gently squeeze the mould to allow the jelly to come away from the sides. Invert each jelly onto a small plate, then drizzle with olive oil, season with salt and serve.

LOBSTER SALAD WITH WAXY POTATOES, PRESERVED ARTICHOKES AND TARRAGON MAYONNAISE

Serves 2

Here I've used the rest of the lobster that wasn't made into sashimi (see page 177) on Christmas Day. Even though I've declared sashimi my favourite way to eat lobster, I love it in a salad like this, particularly if it's freshly cooked. If you don't grow French tarragon, then add tarragon vinegar to your Christmas shopping list and use this instead of verjuice in the mayonnaise as the flavour is perfect with lobster. I added preserved artichokes because I happened to receive a beautiful bottle of Italian artichokes in extra virgin olive oil from Sagittario in Tuscany as a Christmas gift. Leave out the artichokes if you can only find ones preserved in vinegar as they will spoil the dish. Now this jar of artichokes is finished, in future – if I have the time – in November I'll preserve the last of my home grown artichokes, and use these instead.

400 g waxy potatoes, scrubbed
1 tablespoon finely grated lemon zest
1 teaspoon lemon juice
10 sorrel leaves, shredded (if unavailable, use rocket)
3 artichokes preserved in extra virgin olive oil, cut into quarters
sea salt and freshly ground black pepper

POACHED LOBSTER
½ cup (125 ml) verjuice
2 cups (500 ml) water
1 teaspoon Pernod

20 g unsalted butter
1 sprig French tarragon
1 small raw lobster tail (about 170 g)

TARRAGON MAYONNAISE
3 free-range egg yolks
½ teaspoon Dijon mustard
2 tablespoons verjuice
2 teaspoons lemon juice
1 tablespoon water
2 teaspoons chopped French tarragon
sea salt and freshly ground white pepper
1 cup (250 ml) extra virgin olive oil

1 To make the mayonnaise, place the egg yolks, mustard, verjuice, lemon juice, water, tarragon, 1 teaspoon salt and ¼ teaspoon pepper in a food processor and blend to just combine. While the motor is running, slowly drizzle in the olive oil until the mixture has emulsified, taking care not to add the oil too fast or the mayonnaise will split. Taste and adjust the seasoning if needed. Transfer the mayonnaise to an airtight container and refrigerate until needed. (Makes 1½ cups [450 g]. Leftover mayonnaise will keep closely covered with plastic film in an airtight container in the fridge for up to 3 days.)

2 Place the potatoes in a saucepan, then cover with cold water. Bring to the boil over high heat, then cook until tender when pierced with a sharp knife. Drain and leave until just cool enough to handle, then peel by hand, transfer to a bowl and roughly mash. Set aside to cool to room temperature.

3 To poach the lobster, place the verjuice, water, Pernod, butter and tarragon in a heavy-based saucepan over low–medium heat. Bring to a very gentle simmer, add the

lobster tail and cook for 3 minutes, then flip and cook for a further 3 minutes or until just cooked through; the exact time will depend upon the thickness of the tail. Transfer the lobster to a plate, then leave to rest for 5 minutes or until cool enough to handle. Shred the meat into bite-sized pieces. Set aside.

4 Add 2 tablespoons of the mayonnaise to the potato and gently fold together until well combined, then transfer to a serving bowl.

5 Mix the lobster, lemon zest, lemon juice, sorrel, artichoke and another 2 tablespoons of the tarragon mayonnaise in a bowl, then adjust the seasoning. Place on top of the potato mixture, add a final grinding of pepper and serve.

WARM BRIOCHE AND ICE-CREAM SANDWICHES

Serves 6

I've always wanted to try this, having read about the Sicilian practice of serving warm brioche with gelato for breakfast some twenty years ago. It wasn't until my second, and fairly recent, trip to this fascinating island that I visited a bar in Zambucca that offered warm brioche and a selection of gelato. I was so excited to finally taste this, and thought it a great idea to have the components on hand for a casual, no-fuss day like Boxing Day, when anyone might drop in. For me, it's all about using what I have on hand. I've found that brioche freeze beautifully and I always have a stash of my ice creams in the freezer, but if there was a gelato maker in the Barossa, I'd have used that instead – the choice is yours.

¼ cup (60 ml) lukewarm water
1 × 7 g sachet or 1½ teaspoons dried yeast
   (or 15 g fresh yeast)
3 teaspoons caster sugar
220 g plain flour, plus extra for dusting
salt
3 large free-range eggs (65 g each), beaten
185 g unsalted butter, divided into
   sixths, at room temperature
your favourite ice cream or gelato
   and icing sugar, to serve

GLAZE
1 free-range egg white
1½ tablespoons milk

1 Place the warm water, yeast and 1 teaspoon of the caster sugar in a small bowl and stir to combine and dissolve the sugar. Set aside for 10 minutes or until the mixture is foamy.

2 Place the flour, remaining sugar and 1 teaspoon salt in a large bowl and add the yeast mixture and egg. Using your hands, mix to form a dough, squeezing and pulling the dough upwards, for 20 minutes or until it becomes elastic. The dough will be very moist. (You can use an electric mixer fitted with a dough hook, if you like.)

3 Using your hands, incorporate the butter one piece at a time, rubbing it in with your fingers; each new piece should be added only when the last has been absorbed. The dough will be sticky, but should retain its elasticity.

4 Place the dough in a clean bowl, cover with a tea towel and set aside in a draught-free area for 4 hours or until tripled in size. (The dough does not need to be in a warm place. If the dough looks very greasy, this means the butter has melted, so place it in the fridge from time to time to cool.)

5 Turn the dough out onto a lightly floured workbench, then shape it into a 30 cm × 15 cm rectangle. Fold the dough into three, folding each third over the other to form a 15 cm × 10 cm rectangle. Press out again, and repeat folding it into three. Put the dough back into the bowl, then cover and leave for 1½ hours or until doubled in size.

6 Shape the dough into a 15 cm disc, then place it on a plate and refrigerate, uncovered, for 30 minutes: this is to make the dough firm enough to shape.

7 Shape the dough into an 18 cm-long log, then divide into six 3 cm long pieces, shaping each piece into a ball. Place the balls on a baking tray lined with baking paper and set aside for 30 minutes or until almost doubled in size.

8 Meanwhile, preheat the oven to 220°C fan-forced (240°C conventional).

9 For the glaze, whisk the egg white and milk together. Just before baking, brush the top of each brioche with the glaze.

10 Bake the brioche for 15 minutes, then reduce the oven temperature to 180°C fan-forced (200°C conventional) and bake for another 15 minutes or until they are golden and sound hollow when tapped on the base. Cool on a wire rack for 10 minutes.

11 Cut in half, then serve warm with scoops of your favourite ice cream or gelato wedged in between, topped with a dusting of icing sugar.

Dried
apricot
pavlova

DRIED APRICOT PAVLOVA

Serves 10–12

If you've read any of my cookbooks you will know I am a self-confessed non sweet-tooth. Although I enjoy putting desserts together, especially when they involve fruit, they are very much a special occasion thing in our household. I rarely order dessert in a restaurant, much preferring savoury over sweet.

The exception to this is pavlova, which is ironic considering how sweet they are; however, I can't resist them. I tend to hide any leftover pavlova in the back of the fridge so only I know it's there – selfish, I know, but I find it even more addictive after it's gone all squidgy in the fridge. Having declared all of that, my favourite pavlovas are ones with a sweet and sour component. The piquancy of creme fraiche takes away from the sweetness. Although I use the Dried Apricots in Verjuice Syrup I make for the Farmshop, which you can buy online from maggiebeer.com.au, this recipe allows you to make these apricots yourself. This is perfect for Boxing Day, when I have lots of egg whites leftover from making mayonnaise in the fridge needing to be used up. It's an absolute doddle to prepare the meringue – it can even be baked in advance and frozen, making this a simple assembly job. Although, I grant you, the oven will need to be turned on to roast the nuts.

8 free-range egg whites
  (from 59 g eggs)
salt
2 cups (440 g) caster sugar
2 tablespoons cornflour
2 tablespoons verjuice
1 cup (100 g) flaked almonds
2 cups (500 ml) thickened cream
2 cups (500 ml) creme fraiche

APRICOT FILLING
500 g dried apricots
1 cup (250 ml) verjuice
1 cup (250 ml) water
2 tablespoons honey
2 stems rosemary

1 Preheat the oven to 140°C fan-forced (160°C conventional). Line two baking trays with baking paper.

2 Place the egg whites and a pinch of salt in the bowl of a clean and dry electric mixer and whisk until soft peaks form. With the motor running, gradually sprinkle in one-third of the caster sugar at a time, whisking well until the mixture is stiff, glossy and tripled in volume; it should stand up and not move when the beaters are lifted and turned upside-down. To check the sugar has dissolved, rub the meringue between your fingers – if it feels at all grainy, continue to beat. Add the cornflour and verjuice and beat until just combined.

3 Divide the meringue mixture in half. Place one half on each prepared tray and shape into a 30 cm × 24 cm × 2 cm rectangle. Place in the oven immediately and bake for 40–45 minutes or until crisp on the outside and marshmallow-y inside.

4 Turn off the oven and leave the meringues to cool completely in the oven with the door ajar (wedge the oven door open with a wooden spoon).

5 Once the meringues have been removed from the oven, preheat it to 200°C fan-forced (220°C conventional). Roast the almonds on a baking tray for 4 minutes or until light golden, checking them frequently to make sure they don't burn. Set aside.

6 To make the apricot filling, place the dried apricots in a microwave-proof bowl, then pour over the verjuice and water and cover with plastic film. Microwave on the defrost setting for 4 minutes to plump and soften the apricots. (My microwave is 1100 watts; this time will vary if you have a lower wattage microwave.) Remove from the microwave, then strain and reserve the verjuice mixture and set the apricots aside.

7 Place the reserved verjuice mixture, honey and rosemary in a large heavy-based frying pan over low–medium heat and gently simmer for 1–2 minutes or until slightly reduced. Add the apricots and cook over low heat for 3 minutes or until the apricots are soft. Transfer the apricots to a roasting pan lined with baking paper or a bowl and set aside. Increase the heat to medium–high and simmer the syrup for 2 minutes or until it starts to bubble and turns deep golden. Immediately remove from the heat and pour over the apricots, then set aside to cool.

8 Using hand-held electric beaters, whisk the cream until medium–soft peaks form. Add the creme fraiche and whisk for another 30 seconds. Spoon half of the cream mixture on top of one layer of the meringue, then top with the second layer of the meringue. Spoon the remaining cream mixture on top. Arrange the apricots and cooled almonds on top of the cream, then drizzle with the apricot syrup.

9 Cut into slices and serve.

APRICOT FOOL

Serves 4

Apricots come into season very close to Christmas in the Barossa, so usually someone has ripe ones at the last farmers' market before Christmas. All the farmers hope their apricots don't ripen on Christmas Day itself, of course, but this isn't easy to control as, like most things in farming, the weather decides for you. Apricots grown in the Barossa with limited water and picked ripe from the tree boast such an amazing flavour it's hard to replicate with apricots picked before they are ripe for long-distance transporting. Now with our own orchard I realise that, even if the harvest is late, I can always find ripe fruit on one of our trees, given we have several thousand! This dish is so simple that if you can't get farm-picked ripe apricots I suggest using reconstituted good-quality dried ones instead.

2 tablespoons flaked almonds
1 cup (250 ml) thickened cream
1 cup (250 ml) creme fraiche

APRICOTS IN SYRUP
½ cup (125 ml) verjuice
¼ cup (90 g) honey
1 stick cinnamon
500 g firm, but ripe apricots
   (about 8), halved

1 To make the apricots in syrup, place the verjuice, honey and cinnamon stick in a large heavy-based saucepan over medium–high heat. Bring to the boil, then simmer for 5 minutes. Add the apricots and reduce the heat to low, then simmer for 10 minutes or until they have softened but still hold their shape (the cooking time will depend on the ripeness of the apricots). Discard the cinnamon stick. Transfer the apricots to a plate, then simmer the syrup over high heat for 1 minute or until thickened and reduced by half. Set aside to cool.

2 Meanwhile, preheat the oven to 200°C fan-forced (220°C conventional). Roast the almonds on a baking tray for 4 minutes or until light golden, checking them frequently to make sure they don't burn. Set aside to cool.

3 Whisk the cream until soft peaks form, then fold through the creme fraiche and half of the cooled syrup.

4 Divide half of the cream mixture and half of the apricots among 4 serving glasses. Top with the remaining cream mixture and apricots, then chill in the fridge for 30 minutes.

5 Drizzle a little of the reserved syrup over each glass, then sprinkle with the roasted almonds and serve.

PEACH AND BERRY JELLY TRIFLE

Serves 8–10

I have loved trifle ever since I was a child. Was it being allowed to eat right down to the bottom of the bowl where I'd find the sherry-soaked cake, or was it the jelly and fruit? Whatever it was, I've never tired of eating trifle. This version is a bit fancy, I grant you, but it's easily within the province of the home cook. And though it was designed to use leftovers, it's a dessert I'd pull out for special occasions too. I like to set this down in the centre of my table so everyone can help themselves – a much more connected way to eat. However, you could always 'deconstruct' the large trifle and make individual serves in parfait glasses. You will need to make the jelly the day before you assemble the trifle to allow time for it to set, then refrigerate the trifle overnight so the flavours can meld.

40 g unsalted butter
6 yellow peaches, cut in half, pitted
1 tablespoon soft brown sugar
12 sponge finger (savoiardi) biscuits
½ cup (125 ml) dry sherry (I use Oloroso)
500 g raspberries or blackberries (depending on the juice used for the jelly)
pouring cream, to serve (optional)

BERRY JELLY
1½ cups (375 ml) unsweetened
    raspberry or blackberry juice
    (available from delicatessens)

60 g caster sugar
3½ × 2 g gold-strength
    gelatine leaves
2 cups (500 ml) cold water

SABAYON
4 free-range egg yolks
¼ cup (55 g) caster sugar
finely grated zest of 1 lemon
2½ tablespoons dry sherry
    (I use Oloroso)
200 ml thickened cream

1 To make the jelly, place the juice and caster sugar in a heavy-based saucepan, then slowly bring to the boil over low heat, stirring frequently to dissolve the sugar. Set aside to cool slightly. Meanwhile, put the gelatine leaves into a bowl with the cold water, then leave to soften for 5 minutes. Squeeze the excess water out of the gelatine leaves and drop them into the just-warm juice mixture, then stir well until the gelatine has dissolved. Pour into a 2 cup (500 ml)-capacity shallow dish (about 18 cm × 12 cm) and refrigerate overnight to set. Cut into bite-sized cubes just before assembling the trifle.

2 Preheat the oven to 220°C fan-forced (240°C conventional).

3 Place the butter in a baking dish and heat in the oven until it has melted and is sizzling. Add the peaches, cut-side up, and sprinkle with the brown sugar, then bake for 10 minutes or until cooked through (the cooking time will depend on the ripeness of the peaches). Set aside until cool enough to handle, then carefully peel off and discard the skins and slice the flesh.

4 To make the sabayon, combine the egg yolks, caster sugar and lemon zest in a heatproof bowl that fits snugly over a pan of simmering water, taking care that the bottom of the bowl does not touch the water. Using hand-held electric beaters, whisk the mixture until thick and almost tripled in volume – when the beaters are lifted the mixture should hold a ribbon over the surface. Continuing to whisk, add a tablespoonful of the sherry at a time, whisking after each addition until the mixture is thick. Cover closely with plastic film and chill in the fridge. Whisk the cream until soft peaks form, then gently fold through the egg yolk mixture.

5 Lay the sponge fingers in the base of a 4 litre-capacity glass serving bowl. Spoon over the sherry, then spread with half of the sabayon. Add the peach slices, then top with the jelly. Top the final layer with the remaining sabayon and finish with the berries. Cover loosely with plastic film and refrigerate overnight for the flavours to meld.

6 Spoon the trifle into bowls, then serve with cream alongside, if liked.

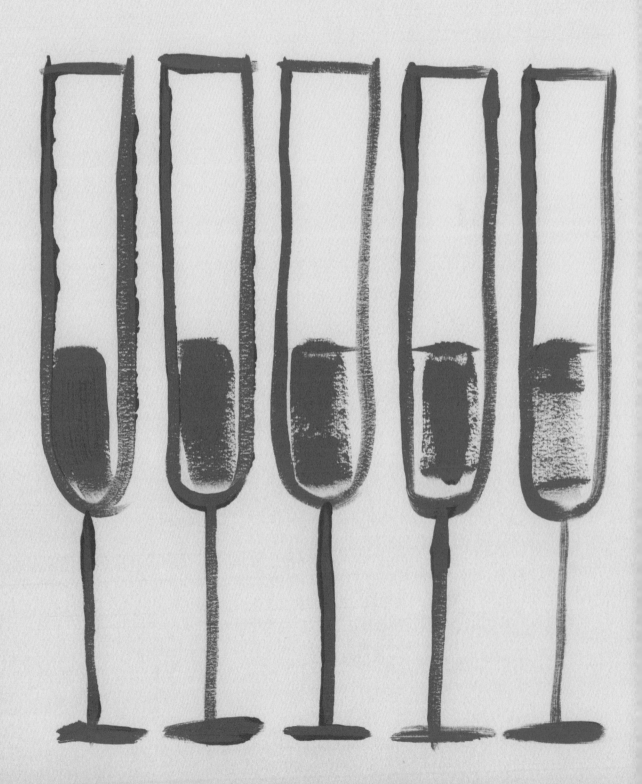

New Year's Eve Dinner*

LUCKILY BY NEW YEAR'S EVE WE'VE HAD A FEW DAYS OF 'NORMAL' eating after Christmas, and all the leftovers have been finished, so we are ready to start on the next round of holiday food. My thinking is that you either belong to the New Year's Eve party or dinner group camp, or you see the first day of the New Year as the time to celebrate, perhaps more sedately with a luncheon for family or friends to ring in the New Year. I honestly don't think I could do both. I've constructed this menu with ease of cooking in mind, then included a special luncheon menu for New Year's Day on pages 279–299 of the next chapter. Each of these meals could easily be worked the other way around if you like – and both have, I hope, an elegant simplicity.

Anyone can have pate at any time, but it's the accompaniments I've used here that take it to another dimension. Besides, I'm a control freak about how you should serve my pate to enjoy it at its best, and the photograph on page 249 illustrates this clearly. Gazpacho is an ideal choice as it tastes even better when made the day before, minimising your stress on the day. I've also given my tips on page 256 for making the ballotine in advance and freezing it, so the rest of this meal won't tax you at all. I was fortunate to find a wonderful jar of honeycomb, which I used over the whole of this festive season, including serving it alongside the walnut bread on pages 272–3. This fantastic product is from Maya Sunny Honey in Ilford, NSW. The bees actually produce the honeycomb inside the 2.5 kg jar – it makes a wonderful statement when added to your table.

For our part, rather than hosting or attending a big New Year's Eve party, we have a tradition of sharing dinner with a group of 16–20 friends, hosted by Tia Schubert and her artist husband Rod. Their home is such a great party house that we often congregate there. Tia assigns each of us an element of the meal to bring, which is a great way to manage having a larger than usual number of people for dinner. Even so, I know Tia still bears the brunt of it all and I haven't yet put my hand up to have the dinner at our place. Of the 40 years we've lived in the Valley, the past 35 New Year's Eves have been spent with this group of friends. Even when we've managed to escape to the beach house for a few days after Christmas, we always return home to the Barossa to see the old year out and welcome the new one in with these friends.

As I'm on the sentimental side, and eternally optimistic, I always have New Year's resolutions. Not that I share them with anyone, or am even successful in carrying them through! However, the intent is always there and somehow it just feels right to start the new year at home.

New Year's Eve Dinner

Menu for 8

Melba toast with my duck and orange pate ~ 248

Gazpacho with sashimi prawn ~ 250

Salad of bitter leaves and grapes ~ 253

Ballotine of Barossa chook ~ 256

Baked peaches with ginger and lemon shortbread ~ 260

Cumquat, almond and chocolate tart ~ 266

Walnut bread with ripe blue cheese and honeycomb ~ 272

MELBA TOAST WITH
MY DUCK AND ORANGE PATE

Serves 8–10

You might think this is cheating, given you have to buy the pate from a shop, however, what better thing to have on hand in the fridge for holiday time . . . I also wanted to take the opportunity to share some simple but important notes for serving one of my pates. The pate contains no preservatives (other than the tiny amount that you would normally also find in wine), so it needs to be kept refrigerated until the last moment before serving. It's even better to present it on an ice bath, as you would for freshly shucked oysters. This not only keeps the pate perfectly, it adds a sense of drama to the table. Also, if the pate gets warm it loses flavour, texture and colour – just like oysters getting warm, and it will be vulnerable to spoiling. As to serving the pate, I know it's indulgent but, as I make it I don't count the cost, I never spread it on toast. Rather, I serve it with a teaspoon for spooning it generously onto the melba toast, as this gives the best flavour and mouth-feel possible. Given the touch of orange in the pate, I love pairing it with my Seville oranges in verjuice syrup, first thinly sliced or cut into fine dice, along with perhaps some cornichons. By the way, a glass of Botrytis wine is the perfect accompaniment.

1 × 120 g tub Maggie Beer Duck
   and Orange Pate
ice cubes
3 slices Maggie Beer Seville Oranges in
   Spiced Verjuice Syrup (optional,
   available from maggiebeer.com.au),
   thinly sliced or cut into fine dice
cornichons, to serve

MELBA TOAST
200 g Walnut Bread (see page 272),
   cut into 2 mm-thick slices
100 g unsalted butter, melted

1 Preheat the oven to 220°C fan-forced (240°C conventional).

2 To make the melba toast, lay the sliced bread on a baking tray. Brush one side of the bread with the melted butter, then bake for 5 minutes or until golden. Transfer the melba toast to a wire rack to cool. Set aside until ready to use.

3 Serve the toast with the pate spooned rather than spread on, with Seville orange (if using) and cornichons alongside.

GAZPACHO WITH SASHIMI PRAWN

Serves 8

Gazpacho is the perfect choice to start off a special summer menu. It is best made up to a day in advance to allow the flavours to meld, then all you need to do is prepare the prawns moments before serving. If you have the chance to buy a box of 'sauce' tomatoes from the farmers' market, then these are ideal here as the flavour of the tomatoes will be the flavour of the gazpacho. I'm always shocked at how inexpensive these really ripe tomatoes are, given that these are how I think we should buy tomatoes for the table, not just for turning into sauce.

6 × 1 cm-thick slices stale sourdough
   bread, crusts removed and broken
   into cubes (to yield 2½ cups)
¼ cup (60 ml) verjuice
3 cloves garlic, crushed
½ cup (125 ml) extra virgin olive
   oil, plus extra for drizzling
⅓ cup (80 ml) red wine vinegar
¾ cup (180 ml) water
1 small bulb fennel, trimmed
   and roughly chopped
1 red capsicum (pepper), seeded
   and roughly chopped
1.5 kg ripe tomatoes, cores removed
   and roughly chopped

1 telegraph (continental) cucumber, peeled,
   seeded and sliced
½ red onion, finely chopped
sea salt and freshly ground black pepper

SASHIMI PRAWN
16 sashimi-quality raw prawns, peeled
   and cleaned, chilled
2 tablespoons extra virgin olive oil
finely grated zest of 1 lemon
chervil leaves, to serve
freshly ground black pepper

1 Place the bread in a bowl and pour the verjuice over to soften (it's only a small amount of liquid so toss the bread around). Transfer the bread mixture to a blender and add the garlic, olive oil, vinegar and ¼ cup (60 ml) of the water, then pulse to combine. Transfer to a large bowl and set aside.

2 Place the fennel and capsicum in the blender and pulse with the remaining ½ cup (125 ml) of water, then add the tomato, cucumber and onion and blend. Return the bread mixture to the blender and pulse to combine. Add salt and pepper to taste, then cover with plastic film and chill for a couple of hours, preferably overnight, to allow the flavours to meld and the bread to swell.

3 Just before serving, prepare the sashimi. Thinly slice the chilled prawns, then place in a bowl. Add the olive oil, lemon zest and chervil and toss to coat. Season with a little pepper.

4 Divide the gazpacho among serving bowls, then spoon an equal quantity of the sashimi prawn into the centre of each bowl. Drizzle with olive oil, then serve.

SALAD OF BITTER LEAVES AND GRAPES

Serves 8 as an accompaniment

This has to be my favourite salad combination of all. It's about the bitterness of the witlof and radicchio leaves and the pepperiness of the rocket in contrast with the sweetness of the grapes. When grapes aren't in season I might replace them with pear, which I've sliced thinly, then drizzled with some verjuice to prevent it from browning – or I even just serve the leaves themselves if neither grapes nor pears are to hand. When it comes to making the vinaigrette, it is worth measuring the ingredients carefully until the balance of flavour becomes second nature. Then it's a matter of only ever tossing the salad with the vinaigrette the moment before you are ready to eat it. My preference is to always finish the main component of the meal before I serve the salad; however, this is a matter of personal choice!

1 small head radicchio, trimmed,
   washed, dried and torn
2 handfuls rocket, trimmed,
   washed and dried
3 heads witlof, leaves separated,
   washed and dried
1 cup (175 g) seedless green grapes
1 cup (180 g) seedless black grapes

VINO COTTO VINAIGRETTE
¼ cup (60 ml) extra virgin olive oil
3 teaspoons red wine vinegar
1 teaspoon vino cotto
sea salt and freshly ground
   black pepper

1 Chill the radicchio, rocket and witlof in a bowl in the fridge for 1 hour before serving.

2 To make the vinaigrette, place the olive oil, vinegar and vino cotto in a bowl and whisk to combine, then season to taste with salt and pepper. Set aside.

3 Add the grapes to the leaves. Only dress the salad with the vinaigrette moments before you wish to eat it.

Ballotine of
Barossa
chook

BALLOTINE OF BAROSSA CHOOK

Serves 8–10 as part of a buffet

When it comes to actually serving family and friends at the dinner table, there is nothing easier than carving a boned, stuffed and rolled chook, or ballotine. I know I often talk about roasting birds or meat on the bone for the best flavour; however, I'm all for ease of serving when it comes to cooking a special dinner for a large group. I can confess to having, at times, boned, stuffed, rolled, and then frozen a chook, weeks before the event to take the pressure off. This works incredibly well, as long as you allow 24 to 36 hours for it to thaw in the fridge, and have used a large, well-brought-up chook. Even so, I'd do this as a back-up and not normal practice. You really need a digital thermometer for this – I think every cook should have one and they are inexpensive. By using the thermometer you can be sure you are taking the chook out of the oven at the perfect temperature. Then it's just a matter of drizzling it with verjuice, then checking the temperature has risen as specified below after 5 minutes out of the oven, and resting it for another 30 minutes – I promise it will retain its heat. It won't be boiling hot, but the perfect temperature to serve.

1 × 1.8–2 kg Barossa or other free-range chicken, boned but left in 1 piece, taking care not to pierce the skin (ask your butcher to do this)
100 g unsalted butter, softened
¼ cup (60 ml) extra virgin olive oil
1 teaspoon vino cotto

CUMQUAT AND PISTACHIO STUFFING
½ cup (25 g) sliced dehydrated cumquats (available from tolleysnurseries.com.au)
2 tablespoons boiling water

¼ cup (35 g) pistachios
40 g unsalted butter
150 g free-range chicken livers
2 tablespoons extra virgin olive oil, plus extra as needed
1 onion, roughly chopped
1½ tablespoons finely chopped rosemary
1 cup (70 g) coarse fresh breadcrumbs, from crustless bread
1½ tablespoons finely chopped lemon thyme
3 tablespoons finely chopped flat-leaf parsley
sea salt and freshly ground black pepper

1 Place the chicken, skin-side down, on a chopping board and gently flatten with a meat mallet so that the meat is of an even thickness all over. Place it on a baking tray, then refrigerate to dry out the skin while you start preparing the stuffing.

2 To make the stuffing, place the cumquats in a heatproof bowl and pour over the boiling water, then set aside to rehydrate for 30 minutes.

3 Meanwhile, preheat the oven to 200°C fan-forced (220°C conventional). Roast the pistachios on a baking tray for 5 minutes or until light golden, checking them frequently to make sure they don't burn. Set aside to cool.

4 Remove the chicken from the fridge and set aside for 30–40 minutes to come to room temperature while you continue with the stuffing. Melt the butter in a large heavy-based

non-stick frying pan over high heat. Add the chicken livers and seal for 90 seconds only on each side. Set aside in the hot pan until cool enough to handle, then carefully cut out the connective tissue, taking care to keep the livers as whole as possible.

5 Heat the olive oil in another non-stick frying pan over medium–high heat. Add the onion, then reduce the heat to low and cook for 20 minutes or until caramelised. Add the rosemary and cook for a further 2–3 minutes, then remove from the heat.

6 Place the breadcrumbs, lemon thyme, parsley, cumquats, pistachios, chicken livers and onion mixture in a large bowl and mix together until well combined, then stir in enough olive oil to just bring the stuffing together (about 1½ tablespoons should suffice). Season to taste with 1 teaspoon salt and a few grindings of pepper.

7 Preheat the oven to 220°C fan-forced (240°C conventional).

8 Place the chicken on a chopping board, skin-side down, with a long side facing you. Spoon the stuffing along the centre of the chicken, making sure the liver pieces are evenly spaced along the length. Starting from the front edge closest to you, roll the chicken over the filling to enclose the stuffing, forming an approximately 45 cm-long × 10 cm-wide log. Truss the rolled chicken with kitchen string at 2 cm intervals along the length to secure it into a compact roll; this ensures the chicken cooks evenly and makes it easier to cut into neat portions for serving. (Alternatively, use skewers to hold the rolled chicken in place while you tie it with kitchen string, then remove the skewers before cooking. It may be helpful to have two pairs of hands to tackle the job – one to hold the rolled chicken and one to truss.)

9 Layer two 70 cm-long sheets of foil, then liberally coat the top layer with the softened butter. Place the chicken lengthways on top, then roll up into a tight parcel, twisting the ends to seal like a bonbon.

10 Place the chicken roll in a dry flameproof roasting pan or large ovenproof non-stick frying pan over high heat, then cook for 7 minutes, turning every couple of minutes and gently pressing down on the foil to seal the chicken evenly.

11 Transfer the pan to the oven and immediately reduce the temperature to 200°C fan-forced (220°C conventional). Roast the chicken for 8 minutes, then turn over and roast for another 8 minutes or until cooked through. The chicken is ready when its internal temperature registers 62°C on a meat thermometer. Remove the chicken from the oven and leave to rest for 5 minutes, then test the internal temperature again; it should register between 67°C and 68°C. Turn the chicken over and rest, breast-side down, for another 20–30 minutes.

12 Meanwhile, remove ¼ cup (60 ml) of the pan juices, then strain off the top layer of fat. Mix the reserved pan juices with the olive oil and vino cotto in a small bowl and set aside.

13 Cut the chicken ballotine into 2 cm-thick slices and serve with the pan juices.

Baked peaches
with ginger
and lemon
Shortbread

BAKED PEACHES WITH GINGER AND LEMON SHORTBREAD

Serves 8

I have to admit perfectly ripe peaches straight from the tree require no more than cutting (and peeling for some – Colin hates peach skin!). However, due to the difficulties of distributing soft stone fruit, often you can only buy peaches that were picked before they were ripe. In this case, baking is the best way to bring out the most flavour possible. If you like, make the shortbread dough a couple of days ahead of time, then wrap it in plastic film, ready to slice off and bake as you need it. It also freezes well.

4 large ripe, but firm yellow peaches
150 g unsalted butter, chopped
1 tablespoon soft brown sugar
2 tablespoons glacé ginger
⅔ cup (70 g) slivered almonds
pouring cream, to serve

GINGER AND LEMON SHORTBREAD
125 g unsalted butter, cut into
   cubes and softened
40 g caster sugar
pinch of salt
½ teaspoon vanilla extract
1 cup (150 g) plain flour, plus extra
   for dusting
finely grated zest of 1 lemon
¼ cup (55 g) glacé ginger, finely chopped

1 To make the shortbread, combine the butter, caster sugar, salt and vanilla in the bowl of an electric mixer with a paddle attachment and beat until well combined, taking care not to over-mix. Sift the flour into the bowl and mix on low speed until well combined. Stir in the lemon zest and ginger.

2 Transfer the dough to a lightly floured workbench and roll into a 14 cm log, then roll into an oval shape about 6 cm long × 3 cm wide. Wrap the dough in plastic film. Refrigerate for at least 2 hours or until firm (or for up to 2 days).

3 Preheat the oven to 180°C fan-forced (200°C conventional). Line 2 baking trays with baking paper.

4 Cut the dough into 5 mm-thick oval-shaped slices, then place on the prepared trays, leaving room between them to allow them to spread. Bake for 10 minutes or until the edges are golden. Remove from the oven and leave to cool on the trays for 5 minutes, then transfer to wire racks to cool completely. The shortbread will crisp as they cool. Leftovers can be stored in an airtight container for up to 1 week. (Makes about 25.)

5 Preheat the oven to 200°C fan-forced (220°C conventional).

6 Cut the peaches in half, then remove the stones. Place 90 g of the butter on a baking tray in the oven for 2 minutes or until melted and sizzling. Place the peaches, cut-side down, on the baking tray, then sprinkle with the brown sugar. Bake for 5 minutes, depending on their ripeness, or until tender. Set aside to cool.

7 Using a teaspoon, make a little hollow in each peach half, reserving 1½ tablespoons of the pulp. Drain the pulp and transfer it to a food processor, then add the glace ginger, almonds and remaining butter and blend until the almonds are finely chopped and the mixture has combined.

8 Increase the oven temperature to its highest setting – usually 240°C or 250°C (fan-forced and conventional).

9 Spoon the almond mixture evenly into each peach cavity, then place, cut-side up, on the tray and bake for 15 minutes or until the stuffing is golden.

10 Serve the peaches with the ginger and lemon shortbread and cream alongside.

Cumquat,
almond
and
chocolate
tart

CUMQUAT, ALMOND AND CHOCOLATE TART

Serves 12–16

This is an incredibly rich dessert so don't be over-generous with your serves. If you were looking for an easier way and decided to prepare this in advance, you could make all but the chocolate ganache the day before. However, if you do this, refrigerate the tart overnight, then cover it with foil and leave it to come to room temperature before serving. Then it's a matter of making and adding the ganache, then leaving the tart in a cool place for the ganache to set for a few hours at room temperature. As much as glace cumquats are the star of this dessert, you could use any glace fruit you love – just be aware that the bittersweet character of cumquat is a counterpoint to the richness of the tart.

1¼ cups (200 g) blanched almonds
⅔ quantity Sour-cream Pastry (see page 100)
120 g unsalted butter, softened
⅔ cup (150 g) caster sugar
2 free-range eggs, plus 1 free-range egg yolk
1 tablespoon plain flour
2 tablespoons cumquat brandy or dry sherry
½ cup (85 g) sliced dehydrated cumquats
   (available from tolleysnurseries.com.au),
   chopped, plus ¼ cup (40 g) extra, to serve

CHOCOLATE GANACHE
320 ml thickened cream
240 g dark couverture chocolate
   (70% cocoa solids), finely chopped
2 tablespoons cumquat brandy
   or dry sherry

1 Preheat the oven to 200°C fan-forced (220°C conventional). Roast the almonds on a baking tray for 5 minutes or until light golden, keeping an eye on them as they burn easily. Set aside to cool completely, then process in a food processor until finely ground.

2 Roll out the pastry on a floured workbench until it is 2.5 mm thick, then use to line a 24 cm-wide × 4 cm-deep tart tin with a removable base. Trim off the excess pastry with a small sharp knife, leaving 5 mm overhanging to allow for shrinkage during cooking. Chill for 10 minutes before baking. Prick the pastry base with a fork, then line with baking paper and baking beads, beans or rice.

3 Increase the oven temperature to 210°C fan-forced (230°C conventional).

4 Blind bake the pastry shell for 10–15 minutes, then remove the baking paper and weights and bake for a further 5–7 minutes or until pale-golden and dry. To inhibit the base of the shell from bubbling up, gently push it down with a clean tea towel. Set aside.

5 Reduce the oven temperature to 180°C fan-forced (200°C conventional).

6 Place the butter and caster sugar in the bowl of an electric mixer and beat until pale and creamy, then add the eggs and yolk, one at a time and beating well after adding each one. Add the flour and brandy or sherry and combine well. With the motor running, slowly add the ground almonds and beat until well combined. Fold through the chopped cumquats.

7 Spoon the almond mixture into the tart case and smooth the surface. Bake for 35 minutes or until the centre is just cooked. Set aside to cool.

8 Meanwhile, to make the chocolate ganache, place the cream in a small heavy-based saucepan and bring just to the boil. Place the chocolate in a heatproof glass mixing bowl, pour the cream over and leave to stand for 3 minutes, then swirl the mixture around with a spoon to melt the chocolate. Stir in the brandy or sherry. Leave to cool for 10 minutes, then pour the chocolate ganache over the cooled tart and smooth the surface with a flexible spatula.

9 Do not refrigerate, but leave in a cool place for the ganache to set. Place the extra cumquats in the centre of the tart. Cut into thin slices as this is incredibly rich, then serve.

Walnut bread
with ripe
blue cheese
and
honeycomb

WALNUT BREAD WITH RIPE BLUE CHEESE AND HONEYCOMB

Makes 2 loaves

Here's another idea to make this meal special with a minimum of fuss and a maximum of flavour. The walnut bread can be made in advance because it toasts better when it's a little stale. I like to accompany it with a good Australian blue cheese, gorgonzola piccante or Bleu de Lacqueuille, as I've done here – just be sure to bring it to room temperature before serving. (Let common-sense reign here as 20 minutes in a cool place will be sufficient on a 43 degree-Celsius day, which isn't out of the question during a Barossa summer!) I matched this with honeycomb rather than honey, as the texture of the honeycomb is as important as its sweetness to contrast with the piquant creaminess of the ripe cheese. If you can't get any honeycomb, a tub of my quince paste would work beautifully too.

400 g top-quality creamy blue cheese
200 g honeycomb

WALNUT BREAD
2½ cups (250 g) walnuts
¾ cup (180 ml) full-cream milk,
   plus 2 tablespoons extra
15 g fresh yeast (or 1 × 7 g sachet or
   1½ teaspoons dried yeast)
½ teaspoon caster sugar

2 tablespoons warm water
1⅓ cups (200 g) plain flour, plus extra
   for dusting
⅔ cup (100 g) wholemeal plain flour
50 g rye flour
sea salt
3 free-range egg yolks, plus 1 free-range
   egg white
2 tablespoons walnut oil, plus extra
   for greasing

1 Preheat the oven to 200°C fan-forced (220°C conventional). To make the walnut bread, roast the walnuts on a baking tray for 8 minutes or until light golden, checking them frequently to make sure they don't burn. Wrap in a clean tea towel, then rub to remove the skins. Set aside to cool.

2 Heat the ¾ cup (180 ml) milk in a small heavy-based saucepan until lukewarm, then set aside.

3 Mix the yeast, caster sugar and warm water in a small bowl, stirring to form a paste, then leave for 10 minutes or until foamy.

4 Combine the flours with 2 teaspoons salt in the bowl of an electric mixer with a dough hook. Whisk the egg yolks in a small bowl, then stir in the walnut oil. Pour the egg yolk mixture into the centre of the flour mixture, then add the yeast mixture.

5 With the mixer on low speed, slowly add the warm milk, mixing until it is incorporated and a soft dough forms. Add the walnuts.

6 Turn the dough out onto a lightly floured workbench and knead for 5 minutes. Brush the mixing bowl with a little more walnut oil and return the dough, rolling it around

the bowl to coat with the oil. Place a piece of plastic film loosely over the surface of the dough, then set aside for 2 hours or until the dough has doubled in size.

7 Turn the dough out onto a floured workbench and knead for a minute or two, then shape into two 23 cm × 10 cm logs. Leave to rise again on a baking tray dusted with flour for 10–15 minutes.

8 Preheat the oven to 200°C fan-forced (220°C conventional).

9 Whisk together the egg white and 2 tablespoons milk and brush over the surface of the dough.

10 Bake the bread for 10 minutes, then reduce the oven temperature to 180°C fan-forced (200°C conventional) and bake for another 15 minutes or until the loaves are dark golden and the bases sound hollow when tapped.

11 Turn out onto wire racks to cool.

12 Serve the bread with the creamy blue cheese and honeycomb alongside.

New Year's
Day
Lunch.

Welcome to

✝ to

Bar...
Far...
Ma...

Christmas
Market
22 + 29 Decem...
730 - 11³⁰ A...

Happy New Year everyone!

RMIT

I HAVE TO ADMIT THIS MENU FOR NEW YEAR'S DAY IS even simpler to execute than the one for New Year's Eve on pages 243–273. This is on the basis that some of you may be adventurous enough to host both events!

Probably the most difficult thing about this whole meal is ensuring the freshness of the kingfish for the sashimi. As I mention on page 284, your ability to get super-fresh kingfish for New Year's Day will depend on whether, that year, the day before is a trading day, which means you'll be able to buy it from a good fishmonger. When it comes to the beef fillet, you could easily purchase it up to a week in advance as it will be in cryovac, which keeps it so well. When bringing the fillet to room temperature before cooking, take it straight out of the cryovac and place it on a clean plate or tray to allow the strange smell of the wrapping to dissipate, making sure you don't include any blood from the cryovac. Then it's a matter of roasting a few vegetables, making the tomato salad (see page 288) and pulling together the tarte tatin (see page 299). For me, when making this tart, the pastry will always be taken from the freezer – without any embarrassment, given the quality of our local Carême butter puff pastry. This tart is all about making the most of the season. It could just as easily include fresh apricots or peaches instead of nectarines, so rather than being totally fixed on using these, go with the flow and be seduced by the best fruit that is on offer.

New Year's Day Lunch

Menu for 8

Sashimi of kingfish with umeboshi ~ 284

Heritage tomato salad ~ 288

Roasted vegetable salad ~ 293

Slow-cooked fillet of beef ~ 296

Nectarine tarte tatin ~ 299

SASHIMI OF KINGFISH WITH UMEBOSHI

Serves 8 as a starter

I first tried something similar to this on my first visit to Southern Ocean Lodge, where the kingfish was served with an indefinable flavour I loved. Intrigued, I asked the chef at the time what he used and he mentioned the Japanese salty plum, umeboshi, along with balsamic vinegar. I took up the idea and the outcome is this dish, although I've used my vino cotto instead of balsamic. I can just as easily prepare this for eight people as 150, thanks to a trick my product development chef, Chris Wotton, showed me. You simply slice all the sashimi in advance, layering each serve in a circular fashion between sheets of plastic film – such a great 'truc' as they say in professional kitchens. When planning this for New Year's Day, consider which day of the week it falls on, as the day before will need to be a trading day so you can get very fresh, super-chilled fish – vital for sashimi. I order a trimmed fillet for sashimi and, whilst I don't mind a bit of the bloodline showing as this indicates freshness, I trim off all but the smallest amount.

1 × 780 g sashimi-grade kingfish fillet,
   skin-on, trimmed of bloodline, if desired
110 g umeboshi (Japanese salty sour plums),
   pitted and finely chopped (to yield 80 g)
2 spring onions, green sections only, finely
   chopped (to yield 4 tablespoons)

1 tablespoon vino cotto
1 tablespoon extra virgin olive oil,
   plus extra for drizzling
sea salt
finely chopped chives, to serve

1 Holding onto the skin, thinly slice the kingfish with a sharp flexible knife. Lay each slice on a large piece of plastic film, slightly overlapping them in a concentric circle to form a round. Cover with another piece of plastic film and refrigerate until ready to serve.

2 Place the umeboshi, spring onion, vino cotto and olive oil in a bowl. Mix together well, then taste and season with a little salt, if desired (umeboshi is quite salty).

3 Just before serving, remove the top layer of plastic film, then carefully flip the kingfish onto a large serving plate and remove the bottom layer of plastic film. Spoon the umeboshi mixture into a mound in the centre of the kingfish, then sprinkle with chives, drizzle generously with olive oil and season with salt. Serve at once.

HERITAGE TOMATO SALAD

Serves 8 as an accompaniment

How wonderful that we have such easy access to heritage tomato seeds (and other fruit and vegetables) through suppliers such as The Diggers Club, Eden Seeds, and The Italian Gardener, to name a few. This makes such an enormous difference to home gardeners like me as it means we don't have to rely on the more commercial varieties of seedlings available in big nurseries (although I admit I've seen a huge improvement in this over the last few years). There are so many different shapes, sizes and colours of heritage tomatoes to choose from and, whilst they all have different characteristics, flavour is the key. Tomatoes like this need nothing more than a drizzle of extra virgin olive oil, a sprinkle of salt and pepper and perhaps a little basil to make a perfect dish. I was so excited to see just this most recent summer, fruit and vegetable brokers offering boxes of mixed heritage tomatoes through commercial channels – a real breakthrough for the food industry.

1 kg heritage tomatoes (use as many different colours and sizes as you can find)
⅓ cup (80 ml) extra virgin olive oil

sea salt and freshly ground black pepper
100 g fior di latte
small handful basil leaves

1 Cut the tomatoes into slices and wedges so you have a variety of shapes.

2 Drizzle with ¼ cup (60 ml) of the olive oil, then season with salt and pepper and gently mix together. Set aside for 20 minutes.

3 Tear the fior di latte into bite-sized pieces and place in a bowl, then drizzle with the remaining olive oil and season with salt and pepper.

4 Mix the tomatoes and fior di latte together in a large shallow bowl, then scatter with the basil. Serve.

Roasted vegetable salad

ROASTED VEGETABLE SALAD

Serves 8 as an accompaniment

The selection of vegetables used here was based purely on what was in my garden at the time – it's just to show that roasting vegetables need not always be about peeled and cut potato, pumpkin and carrot. This also translates beautifully to cooking on the barbecue – all you need to do then is add a post-cooking marinade whilst the vegetables are still warm, then serve them at room temperature. If serving this alongside the roast beef on page 296, as I have done, an aioli (see page 330) or herb mayonnaise would make a great addition.

4 red onions, unpeeled, cut into
   8 wedges each
¾ cup (180 ml) extra virgin olive oil,
   plus extra for drizzling
sea salt
1 tablespoon vino cotto
12 small beetroot, trimmed

6 purple carrots, peeled
6 carrots, peeled
100 g unsalted butter, chopped and softened
3 zucchini (courgettes), thinly
   sliced lengthways
roughly chopped flat-leaf parsley,
   to serve

1 Preheat the oven to 200°C fan-forced (220°C conventional).

2 Place the onion in a roasting pan, then drizzle generously with olive oil and season with 2 teaspoons salt. Roast for 30 minutes or until burnished. Leave to cool, then peel off and discard 1 layer of the skin only and drizzle with vino cotto. Set aside.

3 Cook the beetroot in a saucepan of salted boiling water for 25–30 minutes or until cooked through when tested with a skewer. Drain, then set aside to cool. Slip the skins off, then cut in half lengthways. Place on a baking tray, scatter with knobs of the butter, drizzle with olive oil and sprinkle with salt.

4 Meanwhile, cook the purple carrots and regular carrots in separate saucepans of salted boiling water for 12 minutes or until almost cooked through. Set aside to cool, then cut in half lengthways. Place on a baking tray, then scatter with large knobs of the remaining butter, drizzle with olive oil and sprinkle with salt.

5 Place the zucchini on a baking tray, then drizzle with olive oil and season with salt.

6 Roast the zucchini for 20 minutes and beetroot and carrots for 15 minutes or until the carrot and zucchini are turning golden around the edges and all the vegetables are cooked through. Place the onion in the oven for 5 minutes to warm though.

7 Place the roasted vegetables on a serving platter or toss together in a large bowl with a drizzle of olive oil, then add the parsley and serve.

Slow-cooked
fillet of
beef

SLOW-COOKED FILLET OF BEEF

Serves 8 as a main

One of the things I love so much about cooking is that you never stop learning. You learn from so many sources that it's hard at times to pinpoint where that exact piece of knowledge came from. However, I distinctly recall that the idea for roasting beef fillet slowly at a low temperature comes from a small birthday dinner party I attended for a special friend. Kylie Kwong flashed into the apartment, raw beef fillet in hand, then threw it into the preheated oven and left, no doubt back to the stoves at her restaurant, Billy Kwong. Upon Kylie's return four or five hours later, we were treated to the most perfectly cooked piece of beef; rare and pink from one side to the other, it melted like butter in the mouth. How great is a dish that cooks so slowly, needs so little attention and tastes so wonderful?

1 × 1.8 kg beef fillet, trimmed (I used
   a Coorong Angus beef fillet, 1.4 kg after
   trimming and 40 cm long × 6 cm wide)
1 tablespoon juniper berries, lightly crushed
4 × 20 cm stems rosemary, leaves stripped
   and roughly chopped
4 tablespoons roughly chopped thyme
2 tablespoons orange zest, removed in
   long, thin strips
sea salt

½ cup (125 ml) extra virgin olive oil,
   plus extra for rubbing
8 fresh bay leaves
¼ cup (60 ml) vino cotto

VINAIGRETTE
reserved beef resting juices
¼ cup (60 ml) extra virgin olive oil
1 tablespoon vino cotto

1 Trim the sinew from the beef fillet (or ask your butcher to do this for you) and tuck the skinny tail end under the fillet, securing it with kitchen string. Tie the rest of the fillet at 4 cm intervals to form a compact shape; this helps the beef to cook evenly.

2 Mix the juniper, rosemary, thyme, orange zest, 1 tablespoon salt and the olive oil in a baking dish. Add the beef fillet, then rub the marinade mixture all over the beef. Top with the bay leaves, slipping them in a row underneath the string. Cover with plastic film and leave to marinate in the fridge for a couple of hours or overnight, if you can, turning occasionally.

3 Remove the beef from the fridge and leave to come to room temperature (about 1 hour).

4 Preheat the oven to 75°C fan-forced (95°C conventional).

5 Pat the beef dry and place in a roasting pan, then roast for 3–3½ hours or until it feels soft when pressed with a finger and gently springs back to shape, turning halfway through cooking. (The beef fillet should register 60°C on a meat thermometer when it is ready.)

6 Rub a little salt and a splash of olive oil all over the fillet. Heat a large heavy-based frying pan over high heat, then add the beef and sear for 6 minutes, turning until evenly browned on all sides. Transfer the beef to a clean baking dish, then pour the vino cotto over and leave to rest for 20–30 minutes; the fillet will be beautifully pink all the way through.

7 To make the vinaigrette, mix the resting juices from the beef with the olive oil and vino cotto.

8 Cut the beef into thick slices and serve warm or at room temperature with the vinaigrette.

NECTARINE TARTE TATIN

Serves 8

A tarte tatin is a good dish to master as you can use almost any fruit you can think of, and apply the principle to make savoury versions as well, featuring tomatoes, beetroot, golden shallots and more. As much as making pastry is a normal part of my life, when it comes to puff pastry I am spoilt by having ready access to locally made Carême puff pastry, and I always keep a roll of it in my freezer. If you can't find this, please use a butter puff pastry as the flavour will out itself in the end result. And be sure to roast the hazelnuts and rub off their skins to maximise flavour – no shortcuts allowed!

2 tablespoons hazelnuts
extra virgin olive oil, for greasing
¾ cup (165 g) caster sugar
⅓ cup (80 ml) verjuice
80 g unsalted butter, chopped
4 large or 7 small nectarines, cut in half
   and stones removed

4 sprigs lemon thyme
275 g purchased pre-rolled butter
   puff pastry (I use Carême), cut into
   a 25 cm disc
Maggie Beer Vanilla Bean and
   Elderflower Ice Cream, to serve

1 Preheat the oven to 200°C fan-forced (220°C conventional). Roast the hazelnuts on a baking tray in the oven for 5 minutes or until golden, checking frequently as they burn easily. Wrap in a tea towel, then rub to remove the skins. Roughly chop and set aside. Grease a deep 24 cm pie dish with olive oil and set aside.

2 Place the caster sugar and verjuice in a non-stick frying pan over high heat, stirring gently to dissolve the sugar. Cook for 3–4 minutes or until it turns a light caramel colour, then add the butter and continue to cook for another 3–4 minutes or until it turns a dark golden caramel.

3 Place the nectarines, cut-side down, in the caramel, then add the lemon thyme and cook for a further 6 minutes or until the nectarines have softened but still hold their shape. Remove from the heat, then place the nectarines, cut-side up, and syrup in the oiled pie dish, discarding the thyme. Top with the pastry disc and gently tuck it in around the edge to enclose the nectarines.

4 Bake the tart for 35–40 minutes or until the pastry is dark golden and puffed. Remove from the oven and leave to stand for 5 minutes. Carefully invert the tart onto a serving plate.

5 Scatter the tart with roasted hazelnuts, then serve warm or at room temperature with ice cream.

Food for the Beach House

THE ONLY THING I'VE EVER MISSED LIVING IN THE BAROSSA is being by the sea. Much of my young life in the western suburbs of Sydney was spent taking public transport to the beach with my brothers on weekends. That magical combination of surf and sun has been embedded in my psyche ever since. And, even though it has taken almost a lifetime to come off, Colin and I now have our very own place by the sea to run away to.

Going to the beach for me is all about relaxing the moment I walk in the door. It's about having time to go for a walk every morning, reading lots of books, listening to music, swimming, of course, and lovely, simple meals accompanied by beautiful wine. Holidays at the beach should be just that – holidays. However, this doesn't mean that the food should be anything but wonderful; it should just be easy to manage. So Colin and I just put a polystyrene box full of fresh food in the car, along with a basket of vegetables and herbs from the garden. I want to cook and eat simply, so I always hope that the luck of our catch out on our tinny, or the generosity of neighbours, will make up the remainder of our holiday table.

Even though building the beach house has given me the chance to set up my kitchen and pantry from scratch – an absolute dream of mine – after decades of renting, I've had lots of experience putting together the pantry items I couldn't stay at the beach without. The basics must be easy to transport. This wasn't so important when our family beach holidays were only a two or so hour drive away from home and I wanted to fit my favourite cooking paraphernalia in the car boot as well, which I always managed to do. My much-loved frying pans, toastie iron and grill-plate always topped the list. However, after the girls left home we often took our beach holidays further afield, flying interstate to warmer climates during the dead of the Barossa winter to remind ourselves that summer would be back. In either case, first on my list is always a bottle of good-quality extra virgin olive oil. Whilst I know you can buy olive oil just about anywhere these days, it is not all that often it's an Australian olive oil from the current harvest. Other must-haves in my luggage include: sea salt; good peppercorns in my own pepper grinder; small tins of good-quality anchovies; a small bottle of verjuice and vino cotto; an oyster knife; and a chef's knife. And before great coffee was a given, (as long as you search for it), I'd have taken a stovetop coffee maker too.

Whether you pack kitchen items to take with you if driving, or plan to buy locally if flying, there are a few basic ingredients that help so much. For me these include a variety of dried pasta, parmesan, haloumi, almonds, walnuts, pine nuts, raisins, currants, panko crumbs and frozen homemade pizza dough. These are especially welcome when it's a family holiday and you've spent hours out in the sun on the beach with your children or grandchildren, and are so tired that dinner time becomes a matter of feeding children quickly. Armed with these in your pantry, along with lemons and fresh herbs, you'll be able to make the most of your wild catch. Even if you can't catch fish yourself, hopefully you'll be able to buy fresh fish from the local shops, so homemade fish and chips definitely come under the umbrella of beach holiday food.

HALOUMI WITH BABA GHANOUSH
AND POMEGRANATE DRESSING

Serves 6

I first happened across Trevor Hart's silky hand-crafted buffalo haloumi when I was part of the judging panel for the *delicious.* Produce Awards in 2012, and I'd never tasted haloumi like it. The flavour and texture were so outstanding – even raw – that I organised to buy three kilos of it and have it shipped to my home in the Barossa just in time for Christmas. It is available in the eastern states, but don't despair if you can't find it, as any haloumi will translate to this quick, easy recipe. The trick is to cut the haloumi moderately thickly so that it becomes golden brown on both sides without overcooking. Have your guests assembled and ready to eat this as soon as it comes out of the pan. As for the baba ghanoush, each eggplant variety has its own flavour so take the recipe as a starting point, then add the tahini and lemon juice judiciously, tasting it as you go to get the balance right for the eggplant variety you have.

¼ cup (60 ml) extra virgin olive oil
1 tablespoon pomegranate molasses
4 Walnut Flatbreads (see page 310)
400 g buffalo haloumi, cut into
   1.5 cm-thick slices
¼ cup (35 g) plain flour, for dusting
sea salt and freshly ground black pepper
2 tablespoons mint, finely shredded
lemon wedges or halves, to serve

BABA GHANOUSH
1 tablespoon extra virgin olive oil
1 kg (about 2 large) eggplants (aubergines)
3 cloves garlic, peeled
sea salt
2 tablespoons tahini
1 tablespoon natural Greek-style yoghurt
1½–2 tablespoons lemon juice
freshly ground black pepper

1 Preheat the oven to 200°C fan-forced (220°C conventional).

2 To make the baba ghanoush, place the eggplants directly over a medium–high gas burner (or on a barbecue grill-plate) and cook, turning occasionally with tongs, for 20 minutes or until the skins are blackened all over. Transfer to a baking tray, then roast for 15 minutes or until the eggplants are very soft.

3 Place the eggplants in a bowl, then cover with plastic film and set aside for 10 minutes. Peel off the skins and discard (I rub the skins off with paper towel, followed by scraping with a knife). Squeeze out any remaining liquid from the eggplant.

4 Crush the garlic with ½ teaspoon salt by dragging the back of a large knife over it on a chopping board a number of times, then transfer to a food processor. Add the tahini, yoghurt, lemon juice to taste and the eggplant flesh and any juices, then blitz until a thick puree forms. Season to taste with salt and pepper, then transfer to a bowl, cover with plastic film and set aside. (Makes about 2 cups [560 g].)

5 Whisk 1 tablespoon of the olive oil with the pomegranate molasses in a small bowl until combined. Set aside.

6 Heat each flatbread in a large heavy-based frying pan over high heat for 1 minute on each side or until slightly charred and golden. Cut into wedges and set aside.

7 Pat the haloumi dry with paper towel and toss in the seasoned flour, shaking off any excess. Heat the remaining olive oil in a large frying pan over medium heat until hot, then pan-fry the haloumi in batches for 2 minutes on each side or until golden.

8 Drizzle the pomegranate dressing over the baba ghanoush, then scatter with mint. Serve at once with the haloumi, flatbread and lemon wedges or halves alongside.

WALNUT FLATBREAD

Makes 4

This walnut flatbread is so moreish you'll find lots of reasons to make it. By rolling the bread thinner, it will turn out more like a large crisp piece of melba toast, perfect for pate. Or roll the dough a little thicker and use it as the base for pizza, topped with goat's curd and some of the roasted eggplant on page 141. Serve this with the baba ghanoush on page 308 or topped with caramelised onions, soft goat's cheese, fresh herbs and a generous drizzle of extra virgin olive oil.

1 cup (250 ml) full-cream milk
1 × 7 g sachet or 1½ teaspoons dried yeast
2 tablespoons honey
2 cups (300 g) plain flour, plus extra
    for dusting
½ teaspoon ground ginger
1¼ cups (125 g) walnuts, roughly chopped

2 tablespoons extra virgin olive oil,
    plus extra for brushing
1 teaspoon fennel seeds, plus extra
    for sprinkling
finely grated zest of 1 orange
sea salt
⅔ cup (100 g) buckwheat flour

1 Place the milk in a microwave-safe container and microwave on high for 1 minute, then pour into a large bowl. (Alternatively, heat in a small saucepan over medium heat until lukewarm.) Whisk in the yeast, honey and 100 g of the plain flour until well combined. Leave to stand for 15 minutes or until frothy. Add the ginger, walnuts, olive oil, fennel seeds, orange zest and 3 teaspoons salt to the yeast mixture and mix together well.

2 Sift the buckwheat flour and remaining plain flour together, then tip in a pile onto a lightly dusted clean workbench and make a well in the centre. Pour the yeast mixture into the well, then use a fork to slowly incorporate the yeast mixture into the flour. Once all the flour has been incorporated, use your hands to knead into a dough (you may need to use extra flour to dust the workbench and your hands if the dough is slightly tacky). At this stage, the dough should bounce back and be reasonably firm.

3 Divide the dough into quarters. Place on 2 baking trays lightly dusted with flour, cover loosely with plastic film and leave to rest for 20 minutes.

4 Meanwhile, preheat the oven to 180°C fan-forced (200°C conventional).

5 Dust the workbench lightly with flour, then roll out each piece of dough to form a 24–26 cm-wide × 2–3 mm-thick round. Brush the surface of the dough with olive oil.

6 Bake the dough for 15 minutes or until dark-golden brown; the flatbread will feel slightly soft straight out of the oven but will become crisp once it cools. Remove from the oven and place on wire racks to cool. (If you prefer crisper flatbread, then bake for a further 5–10 minutes.)

7 Cut the flatbread into wedges, then snap into pieces and serve.

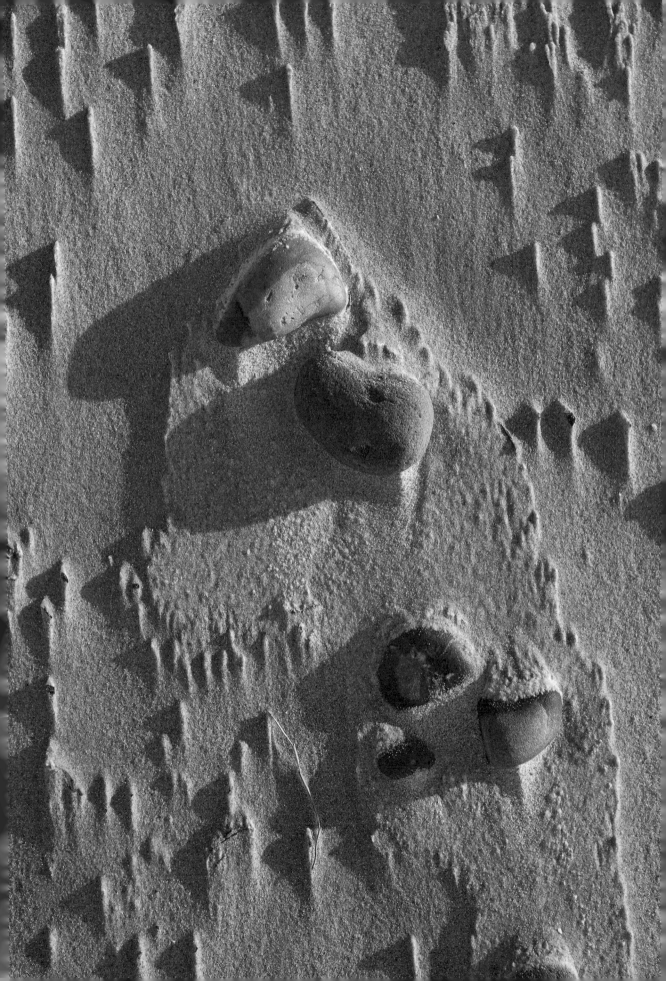

VERJUICE PIZZA DOUGH

Makes 4 × 22 cm pizzas

You don't have to make your pizza dough with verjuice, but I like the slight tang that it gives. If you don't have verjuice on hand, add a squeeze of lemon juice to ¼ cup (60 ml) water instead – it will have the same effect. The great thing about this dough is that you can wrap any balls you don't use in plastic film, then freeze them for up to a couple of months to use another time. Whilst I have a small pizza oven, which gives the most incredible results for cooking any wood-fired food, it is a very recent purchase. Before this was installed, when just cooking casually for ourselves, I used a pizza stone I bought for $10, and preheated in my oven at its highest temperature setting, with great results.

3¼ cups (485 g) plain flour,
   plus extra for dusting
2 teaspoons dried yeast
1 tablespoon sea salt
1 tablespoon caster sugar
¼ cup (60 ml) verjuice

1 cup (250 ml) warm water
2 tablespoons extra virgin olive
   oil, plus extra for greasing
   and drizzling
your choice of topping (see pages 316–20)
polenta, for dusting

1 Place the flour, yeast, salt and sugar in the bowl of an electric mixer fitted with a dough hook. Combine the verjuice, water and olive oil in a jug. Make a well in the centre of the flour mixture, then pour in the verjuice mixture. Mix on the lowest setting for 2 minutes or until the ingredients come together to form a dough. Transfer the dough to a lightly floured workbench and knead for 5 minutes. Roll the dough into a ball and place in a lightly oiled bowl, then cover with plastic film and leave to prove in a warm spot for 1 hour or until doubled in size.

2 Meanwhile, prepare your choice of topping.

3 Divide the dough into quarters and form into 4 balls.

4 Preheat the oven to as high as it will go – generally 240°C or 250°C (fan-forced and conventional).

5 Working with one ball of the dough at a time, place it on a lightly dusted workbench, then flatten it out to form a 22 cm round and drizzle with olive oil. Dust a pizza paddle (or stone) with polenta and place the dough round on top. Place in the very hot oven and bake for 2 minutes or just until the dough starts to puff around the edge and the surface looks dry – the timing will depend on the ferocity of your oven.

6 Proceed with adding your chosen topping to the pizza bases, followed by the final cooking.

PIZZA TOPPING 1:
ARTICHOKE, PANCETTA AND FIOR DI LATTE

Makes enough for 4 pizzas

6 globe artichokes (if young, fresh
   artichokes are not available, use
   artichokes preserved in extra
   virgin olive oil *not* brine or vinegar)
½ lemon
¼ cup (60 ml) extra virgin olive
   oil, plus extra for drizzling
2 tablespoons verjuice

1 quantity Verjuice Pizza Dough
   (see page 315)
16 thin slices round pancetta
1 × 250 g ball fior di latte, torn into pieces,
   drained on paper towel
2 tablespoons roughly chopped
   flat-leaf parsley
sea salt and freshly ground black pepper

1 Cut one-third off the top of each artichoke, then immediately rub it with a cut lemon. Pull away the hard outside leaves and rub the cut surfaces with lemon. Heat the olive oil in a heavy-based frying pan over medium–high heat until hot (but not smoking). Add the artichokes, cut-side down, and cook for 5 minutes. Reduce the temperature to low and continue to cook for 15 minutes or until tender; when you can insert a knife easily through the heart of the artichoke it is cooked. Add the verjuice to the pan and cook the artichokes for another 1–2 minutes, then set aside to cool in the pan. Cut each artichoke in half and remove the hairy choke, if necessary, then tear into pieces.

2 Remove each pre-set pizza base from the oven and top with one-quarter of the torn fior di latte, then scatter over one-quarter of the torn artichokes and top with 4 rounds of pancetta. Drizzle with olive oil, then return to the oven and cook for 2–4 minutes or until dark golden around the edge and base of each pizza and the cheese has melted.

3 Sprinkle each pizza with parsley, drizzle with a final flourish of olive oil and serve at once.

PIZZA TOPPING 2:
RED ONION, ASPARAGUS AND MOZZARELLA

Makes enough for 4 pizzas

2 large red onions, cut into 8 wedges each

2 tablespoons extra virgin olive oil, plus
  extra for drizzling

2 tablespoons vino cotto

16 asparagus spears, bases trimmed

sea salt

1 quantity Verjuice Pizza Dough
  (see page 315)

80 g mozzarella, grated

1 Preheat the oven to 200°C (220°C fan-forced).

2 Place the onion on a baking tray, then drizzle with the olive oil and roast for 20 minutes or until softened and slightly browned around the edges. Drizzle with the vino cotto and set aside.

3 Blanch the asparagus in a saucepan of simmering salted water for 3 minutes or until just tender. Drain and set aside.

4 Remove each pre-set pizza base from the oven and top with one-quarter of the mozzarella, then scatter over one-quarter of the roasted onion and asparagus. Drizzle with olive oil, then return to the oven and cook for 2–4 minutes or until dark golden around the edge and base of each pizza and the cheese has melted.

5 Drizzle each pizza with a final flourish of olive oil and serve at once.

Roasted vegetable and goat's curd pizza

Artichoke, pancetta and fior di latte pizza

Red onion, asparagus and mozzarella pizza

PIZZA TOPPING 3:
ROASTED VEGETABLE AND GOAT'S CURD

Makes enough for 4 pizzas

4 golden beetroot
4 small beetroot
sea salt
140 ml extra virgin olive oil, plus extra
  for drizzling
freshly ground black pepper
4 purple carrots, peeled
2 baby leeks

4 small zucchini (courgettes), cut in half
  lengthways (I was lucky enough to have
  ones with the flowers still attached)
12 cloves garlic
1 quantity Spelt Pizza Dough
  (see page 321)
160 g goat's curd
roughly chopped flat-leaf parsley, to serve

1 Have ready a baking tray large enough to accommodate all the vegetables in one layer.

2 Cook each type of beetroot in a separate pan of boiling salted water for 20 minutes or until tender when pierced with a knife. Drain and set aside until cool enough to handle, then peel off the skins and cut in half. Place on the baking tray and drizzle with 2 tablespoons of the olive oil, then season to taste with salt and pepper.

3 Cook the carrots in a saucepan of boiling salted water for 10 minutes or until tender when pierced with a knife. Drain and set aside until cool enough to handle, then cut in half lengthways. Transfer to the baking tray and drizzle with another 2 tablespoons of the olive oil, then season to taste with salt and pepper.

4 Meanwhile, soak the leeks with the white parts down in a jug of water for 2 minutes to remove all the grit. Cook the leeks in a saucepan of boiling salted water for 10 minutes or until just tender when pierced with a knife. Drain and set aside until just cool enough to handle, then cut in half lengthways. Transfer to the baking tray and drizzle with 1 tablespoon of the olive oil and season to taste with salt and pepper.

5 Preheat the oven to its highest setting – generally 240°C or 250°C (fan-forced and conventional).

6 Place the zucchini, cut-side up, on a small baking tray and add the garlic then drizzle another 2 tablespoons of the olive oil and season with salt. Roast the zucchini and garlic for 5 minutes, then transfer to the tray with the remaining vegetables. Roast all the vegetables for 6–8 minutes or until golden around the edges.

7 Remove each pre-set pizza base from the oven and place one-quarter of the roasted vegetables over the base of each pizza, then top with one-quarter of the goat's curd. Drizzle with olive oil, then return to the oven and cook for 2–4 minutes or until dark golden around the edge and base of each pizza.

8 Sprinkle each pizza with parsley, then drizzle with a final flourish of olive oil and serve at once.

SPELT PIZZA DOUGH

Makes 4 × 22 cm pizza bases

This is a great alternative to the pizza dough on page 315. When I cooked the pizzas for the shoot, I used this dough as the base for the roasted vegetable and goat's curd topping opposite. You could use it with any of the toppings included here, or your favourite pizza toppings.

440 g fine spelt flour, plus extra
   for dusting
2 teaspoons dried yeast
sea salt
⅓ cup (80 ml) extra virgin olive
   oil, plus extra for greasing

1 cup (250 ml) warm water,
   plus 2 tablespoons extra
your choice of topping
   (see pages 316–20)
polenta, for dusting

1 Place the flour, yeast and ½ teaspoon salt in a large mixing bowl and mix together, then make a well in the centre.

2 Add the olive oil and warm water to the well of flour, then, using a fork and stirring in small circles, gradually work the flour mixture into the water and oil until all the flour has been incorporated; this takes about 2 minutes. Transfer the dough to a lightly floured workbench and knead for 5 minutes or until smooth and elastic. Place the dough in an oiled bowl, cover with plastic film, then leave to rest for 1 hour or until doubled in size.

3 Meanwhile, prepare your choice of topping.

4 Preheat the oven to its highest setting – generally 240°C or 250°C (fan-forced and conventional).

5 Divide the dough into quarters and form into 4 balls.

6 Working with one ball of dough at a time, place it on a lightly dusted workbench, then flatten it out to form a 22 cm round and drizzle with olive oil. Dust a pizza paddle with polenta and place the dough round on top. Place in the very hot oven and bake for 2 minutes or just until the dough starts to puff around the edge and the surface looks dry. Remove from the oven.

7 Add your topping of choice, then proceed with the second baking.

Vino cotto-glazed quail
with roasted smoked
and

VINO COTTO-GLAZED QUAIL WITH ROASTED SMOKED TOMATOES AND GARLIC AND FENNEL SALAD

Serves 6

I've borrowed the idea of roasting smoked tomatoes from Neil Perry, after reading his book *Rockpool Bar and Grill*, where he waxes lyrical about them. After making a simplified version in my barbecue, as well as the wood-fired oven at the beach house, I absolutely agree with his rave reviews. I always make extra as I love them the next day drizzled with extra virgin olive oil and scattered with a little torn basil – once you try them I'm sure you'll find many uses for them too. Here I've paired the smoky tomatoes with quail simply brushed with extra virgin olive oil and vino cotto, which results in such perfectly burnished skin that you'll feel so accomplished – as long as you don't overcook them.

6 × 220 g jumbo quail
sea salt and freshly ground black pepper
¼ cup (60 ml) vino cotto
½ cup (125 ml) extra virgin olive oil,
   plus extra for brushing
3 tablespoons roughly chopped rosemary

ROASTED SMOKED TOMATOES AND GARLIC
1 cup (50 g) milled food-grade wood
   shavings (available from specialty
   barbecue stores)
3 tablespoons packed rosemary leaves
6 fresh bay leaves, crushed

1 tablespoon sage leaves
2 tablespoons soft brown sugar
⅓ cup (80 ml) water
2 bunches (300 g) cocktail truss tomatoes
18 cloves garlic, skin-on
1 tablespoon extra virgin olive oil

FENNEL SALAD
2 small bulbs fennel, trimmed and
   cut into quarters
1 tablespoon verjuice
1 tablespoon extra virgin olive oil

1 To smoke the tomatoes and garlic, line a baking tray (I used a 25 cm × 18 cm tray) with foil. Combine the wood shavings, rosemary, bay leaves, sage and brown sugar in a bowl, then spread over the prepared tray. Drizzle over the water; the water will just moisten the mixture so it smoulders to begin with. Remove the barbecue grill-plate and sit the baking tray directly over the burner or coals, then replace the grill-plate.

2 Make a small incision down the side of each tomato and place in a foil baking tray (or baking tray lined with foil). Add the garlic to the tray. Place the baking tray directly on the barbecue grill-plate, then cover with the barbecue lid and heat to high. Smoke the tomatoes and garlic for 20–25 minutes.

3 Just before the tomatoes and garlic are ready, preheat the oven griller to high heat. Remove the tray from the barbecue, then transfer to the oven griller and grill for 5 minutes or until the tomato skins are crisp and slightly blackened. Remove from the griller and set aside until cool enough to handle, then remove the stems, if desired. Set aside at room temperature until ready to serve. (Store leftovers in an airtight container in the fridge for up to 1 week.)

4 Using kitchen scissors, cut along either side of each quail backbone and remove. Open the quail out, skin-side up, and press down firmly with the heel of your hand to flatten. Place the flattened quail in a large baking dish and season inside and out with salt and pepper. Mix together the vino cotto, olive oil and rosemary and use three-quarters of this to marinate the quail. Reserve the remaining marinade. Cover the quail with plastic film and leave to marinate for at least 30 minutes, in the fridge if it's a hot day, turning the quail after 15 minutes and making sure all parts are in contact with the marinade.

5 Preheat a barbecue grill-plate or chargrill pan to high and lightly brush the quail with olive oil. Place the quail, flesh-side down, on the hot grill-plate. Cook the quail for 6 minutes or until almost cooked through (the ribs will seem very charred but this really works). Turn the quail over and cook, skin-side down, for 2 minutes or until the meat is cooked through and the skin is burnished. When the quail is ready the leg meat should pull away easily at the joint. Transfer the quail to a plate and drizzle with the reserved marinade. Cover loosely with foil and leave to rest for 5 minutes.

6 To make the fennel salad, drizzle the fennel with the verjuice and olive oil.

7 Serve the quail with the resting juices spooned over and the roasted tomatoes and garlic and fennel salad alongside.

BRAISED OCTOPUS WITH ROASTED SMOKED TOMATOES, AVOCADO AND AIOLI

Serves 4

I'll let you in on a secret: cooking octopus has some challenges. However, I have a few tips that will ease your path. Even when you request well-tumbled octopus, that is, octopus which has been tenderised in a concrete mixer, it is impossible to tell from looking at it whether this has been done. It's only after a disappointing result that you can tell that it wasn't prepared properly. As a safety net, I use crushed kiwifruit or paw paw to tenderise octopus – but for no longer than an hour or it will break down the flesh too much, making it stringy. This dish is the classic marriage of octopus with avocado and aioli I learnt so long ago from reading Elizabeth David's iconic books.

2 large octopus tentacles (about 1 kg)
2 kiwifruit, peeled and sliced
¼ cup (60 ml) extra virgin olive oil,
    plus extra for drizzling
juice of 1 lemon
1 large or 2 small avocados
1 quantity Roasted Smoked Tomatoes
    (see pages 326–7)
rocket leaves, to serve

AIOLI
2 cloves garlic, crushed
sea salt
2 free-range egg yolks
1 cup (250 ml) extra virgin olive oil
2 tablespoons lemon juice,
    or to taste

1 Place the octopus in a glass bowl, then squeeze the kiwifruit over. Cover with plastic film, then refrigerate for 30 minutes to tenderise.

2 Meanwhile, make the aioli. Pound the garlic and ½ teaspoon salt together with a mortar and pestle to form a paste (or crush together by dragging the back of a large knife over the garlic and salt on a chopping board a number of times). Transfer the garlic paste to a bowl, then add the egg yolks and whisk together. Whisking continuously, slowly incorporate the olive oil a drop at a time until about one-quarter of the oil has been used and the mixture has emulsified. Whisking continuously, slowly add the remaining oil, whisking until the mixture has thickened and emulsified. Whisk in lemon juice to taste, then adjust the seasoning with salt, if desired. Cover closely with plastic film and refrigerate until required. (Makes about 1¼ cups [310 ml].)

3 Dry the octopus tentacles well with paper towel.

4 Heat the olive oil in a deep heavy-based frying pan with a tight-fitting lid over high heat until very hot. Carefully lower the octopus into the pan, then cover with the lid and cook over high heat for 3 minutes. Turn the octopus, then cover with the lid and cook for another 2 minutes. Reduce the temperature to low. (In this initial period, the octopus will become a deep-red colour and exude a lot of juice.) Cook the octopus for another 10 minutes, then check and turn over again. Cook uncovered for a further

5–20 minutes or until tender (the exact time will depend on the age and thickness of the octopus). When the octopus is ready, it should yield to the pressure of your fingers; if it still feels tight, it is undercooked. (However, overcooking will make the octopus thready and lose its texture, so check it frequently.)

5 Remove the octopus from the pan and drizzle with lemon juice. Set aside to cool.

6 Meanwhile, slice the avocado and drizzle with a little lemon juice to prevent it from discolouring.

7 Slice the octopus into bite-sized pieces on the diagonal, then drizzle with olive oil and serve with the avocado, roasted smoked tomatoes, aioli and rocket alongside.

TUNA ROLLS WITH CURRANT AND PINE-NUT FILLING

Serves 6

When I was in Sicily I tried a swordfish dish featuring these wonderful flavours. Back home at the beach house, tuna is virtually on my doorstep, so I've used this instead. During a recent beach stay, my neighbour caught a tuna and presented me with a huge piece – at least two kilos. We enjoyed some as sashimi, I made this with fresh bay leaves from my tree and then preserved the rest – this bounty definitely only happens on beach holidays! The trick here is to pound the tuna pieces so they are evenly thin, then to only cook them for a moment as tuna needs such little cooking to be at its best.

1 large red onion, cut into 12 wedges
⅓ cup (80 ml) extra virgin olive oil
¼ cup (60 ml) vino cotto
1 × 600 g piece tuna (or 3 × 200 g tuna steaks, cut in half widthways), skin-off and bloodline removed, chilled
6 fresh bay leaves
lemon wedges, to serve

CURRANT AND PINE NUT FILLING
2½ tablespoons dried currants
2 tablespoons verjuice
2½ tablespoons pine nuts
2 cloves garlic, crushed
sea salt
large handful flat-leaf parsley leaves
freshly ground black pepper
130 g finely grated aged pecorino
1 tablespoon extra virgin olive oil

1 To make the filling, soak the currants in the verjuice overnight (or for at least several hours). Alternatively, place the currants and verjuice in a microwave-safe container and microwave on low for 2 minutes, then set aside for 20 minutes to reconstitute.

2 Preheat the oven to 180°C fan-forced (200°C conventional). Place the pine nuts on a baking tray and roast for 6–7 minutes or until golden, checking them frequently to make sure they don't burn. Remove and set aside.

3 Crush the garlic with a pinch of salt on a chopping board by dragging the back of a large knife over it a number of times, then add the parsley and chop together well. Add the pine nuts and currants and roughly chop. Transfer to a bowl, then season to taste with salt and pepper. Stir in the pecorino and olive oil until well combined.

4 Increase the oven temperature to 200°C fan-forced (220°C conventional). Line a baking tray with baking paper. Place the onion on the tray, then drizzle with 2 tablespoons of the olive oil and roast for 20 minutes or until softened and slightly browned around the edges, turning halfway through cooking. Drizzle with 1½ tablespoons of the vino cotto and set aside.

5 Keep the tuna chilled until you are ready to use it. Cut the tuna into six 9 cm-wide × 4–5 mm-thick slices. Lay the tuna slices in a row on a chopping board with the narrowest side facing you. Divide the currant filling evenly among the slices, placing

it in a line across the centre of each slice. Starting from the side closest to you, roll up the tuna to enclose the filling, then secure with a toothpick at each end to hold in the filling.

6 Increase the oven temperature to 220°C fan-forced (240°C conventional). Place the tuna rolls in a roasting pan interspersed with the bay leaves and drizzle with the remaining olive oil. Roast for 6–8 minutes or until just cooked. Scatter over the roasted onion and drizzle with the remaining vino cotto, then leave to rest for 2 minutes.

7 Drizzle the tuna rolls with the resting juices, then serve with lemon wedges alongside.

SQUID WITH ANCHOVY
AND PERSIAN FETA STUFFING

Serves 6

Squid can be tricky to cook well, so here are a few simple rules to ensure it is tender every time. Buy squid that was frozen immediately after it was caught as this tenderises it. Either cook it incredibly quickly at a very high temperature or slowly in extra virgin olive oil in a heavy-based pan at such a low temperature that it barely simmers. If you are lucky enough to have access to a wood-fired oven or charcoal grill, then, for me, these are the ultimate tools to use to cook squid. If not, a barbecue (or very hot oven) is great too. Finally, it is important to leave the cooked squid to rest before serving, drizzled with extra virgin olive oil and a generous squeeze of lemon.

⅓ cup (80 ml) extra virgin olive oil, plus
   extra for drizzling
1 large onion, finely chopped
2 cloves garlic, thinly sliced
2 tablespoons verjuice
90 g fine sourdough breadcrumbs
finely grated zest and juice of 1 lemon
handful flat-leaf parsley, roughly chopped

sea salt and freshly ground black pepper
60 g Persian feta, cut into 6 pieces
6 anchovy fillets
6 small–medium whole squid (about
   11–12 cm-long), cleaned, leaving
   tentacles intact
rocket leaves and lemon wedges (optional),
   to serve

1 Preheat the oven to its highest setting – generally 240°C or 250°C (fan-forced and conventional). (Alternatively, heat a barbecue with a hood to its highest temperature.) Line a baking tray with foil.

2 Heat 2 tablespoons of the olive oil in a heavy-based frying pan over medium heat. Add the onion and cook for 8 minutes or until softened and translucent. Reduce the heat to low–medium, then add the garlic and continue to cook for 5 minutes or until the onion begins to gently colour. Deglaze the pan with the verjuice and immediately add the breadcrumbs. Add the lemon zest and parsley, then season to taste with salt and pepper. Place a piece of Persian feta and an anchovy in the cavity of each squid, then fill with the breadcrumb mixture. Seal each opening with a toothpick.

3 Place the squid and tentacles on the prepared tray, then drizzle with a little extra olive oil and sprinkle with salt. Bake the squid for 6 minutes, then turn over and bake for another 2 minutes. (Alternatively, to cook the squid on a barbecue, cook on a hot barbecue flat-plate with the barbecue lid on for 5 minutes, then turn and cook, covered, for another 2 minutes.) Immediately drizzle the lemon juice and remaining olive oil over the squid and leave to rest.

4 Serve warm or at room temperature with the resting juices spooned over and rocket and lemon wedges alongside, if desired.

Squid-ink pasta with poached prawns

SQUID-INK PASTA WITH POACHED PRAWNS

Serves 4 as an entree or 2 as a main

This is the dish I make when I feel like going to a bit more trouble. I love the contrasting colours of the pink prawns on the black pasta. Be very careful to only just cook the prawns. My tip for cooking pasta is to follow the packet instructions, and never rinse it after cooking to cool it. If you wish to cook pasta in advance, it is better to place it on a large dish after draining, drizzle it liberally with extra virgin olive oil and leave it to cool naturally, then warm it briefly in the microwave before serving.

¼ cup (60 ml) extra virgin olive oil,
  plus extra for drizzling
60 g sourdough bread, crusts removed,
  cut into 1 cm-thick slices and torn into
  2 cm pieces
5 litres water
1 tablespoon Pernod
16 raw prawns

sea salt
200 g dried squid-ink spaghetti
3 tablespoons flat-leaf parsley,
  finely chopped
2 tablespoons mint, thinly sliced
1 tablespoon finely grated lemon zest
2 tablespoons lemon juice
1 clove garlic, crushed

1 Heat 2 tablespoons of the olive oil in a heavy-based frying pan over high heat. Add the bread, then cook on all sides, turning for 3–4 minutes or until golden brown all over. Remove from the heat and leave to cool. Transfer to a blender and blend until fine breadcrumbs form.

2 Place 1 litre of the water and the Pernod in a large saucepan, then bring to a simmer. Add 8 of the prawns and poach for 3 minutes or until just cooked, then remove with a slotted spoon, drain and leave to cool. Repeat with the remaining prawns. Remove the heads and tails and devein the prawns, then drizzle with a little olive oil and set aside.

3 Fill a large saucepan with the remaining water, add ¼ cup (55 g) salt and bring to the boil. Cook the pasta following the packet instructions until al dente, then drain.

4 Immediately place the parsley, mint, lemon zest and juice, garlic and remaining 1 tablespoon olive oil in a bowl, add the breadcrumbs, then toss the prawns through to coat evenly in the herb and breadcrumb mixture. Divide the pasta among plates, then evenly top with the prawn mixture. Add a final drizzle of olive oil, then serve at once.

PAN-FRIED SQUID IN BUTTER AND TARRAGON

Serves 4

A couple of things may surprise you here; that is, the use of tarragon and, knowing my great love of extra virgin olive oil, that I've fried the squid in nut-brown butter. Neither way is right nor wrong – I'm simply sharing my favourite way to pan-fry squid. Here are a few tricks I've learnt along the way: have your oven on low heat to keep each batch of squid warm on a paper towel-lined baking tray until all the squid is cooked; squeeze a generous amount of lemon juice over the squid; and have your guests ready to eat this while it is still piping hot.

plain flour, for dusting
sea salt and freshly ground black pepper
3 tablespoons French tarragon, finely
   chopped (if unavailable use 1 tablespoon
   dried tarragon)
2 large whole squid, cleaned with
   tentacles reserved or 2 large squid
   tubes, cut into rings

120 g unsalted butter, chopped,
   plus extra if needed
2 tablespoons extra virgin olive oil
juice of 1 lemon
lemon wedges, to serve

1 Preheat the oven to 130°C fan-forced (150°C conventional). Line a baking tray with paper towel.

2 Season the flour with salt, pepper and the tarragon. Toss the squid in the seasoned flour to coat, shaking off any excess.

3 Melt 60 g of the butter in a frying pan over high heat and cook for 2–3 minutes until nut-brown, adding a splash of olive oil when the butter starts to bubble to prevent it from burning. Add half of the squid so it doesn't crowd the pan and saute over high heat for 2–3 minutes or until the squid is golden brown. Turn out onto paper towel to drain, then squeeze with lemon juice. Transfer to the baking tray, then keep warm in the oven. Wipe the pan clean with paper towel and return to high heat, then repeat with the remaining butter, olive oil, squid and lemon juice.

4 Eat the squid immediately with lemon wedges for squeezing. Absolutely delicious!

pan-fried
squid
in butter
and tarragon

BAKED FLATHEAD WITH GINGER AND VINO COTTO SAUCE AND POTATO SCALLOPS

Serves 4

My love of flathead comes from childhood days spent catching them from a row boat on Sydney Harbour, in the days before we were smart enough to wear hats, let alone sunscreen, and we'd stay out half the day just to be rewarded by that sweet taste of flathead cooked whole in butter. I must confess, too, that potato scallops were my comfort food and secret vice when I was a teenager. I was always the one in my family to order them at the fish and chips shop, as a very special treat, and remember burning my mouth with the first bite of the thick batter-coated scallops wrapped in butcher's paper and newsprint. Having now 'grown up', I make my own scallops with waxy potatoes and a much lighter batter.

1 bunch spring onions, trimmed
1 × 950 g flathead, cleaned and scaled
extra virgin olive oil, for drizzling
1 tablespoon lemon juice
sea salt
1 × 2 cm knob ginger, thinly sliced
4 kaffir lime leaves, crushed
lemon wedges, to serve

POTATO SCALLOPS
4 waxy potatoes (about 450 g)
extra virgin olive oil, for deep-frying
1 quantity Beer Batter (see page 44)
sea salt

GINGER AND VINO COTTO SAUCE
5 golden shallots, finely chopped
1 × 3 cm knob ginger, finely chopped
   (to yield 1 tablespoon)
1 tablespoon vino cotto
⅓ cup (80 ml) verjuice

1 To make the potato scallops, place the potatoes in a saucepan of cold water, then bring to the boil over high heat. Cook the potatoes for 20 minutes or until just cooked. Drain and leave until cool enough to handle. Peel, if desired, then cut into 1 cm-thick slices and set aside.

2 Preheat the oven to 200°C fan-forced (220°C conventional). Line a baking tray with baking paper.

3 To make the sauce, place the shallot, ginger, vino cotto and verjuice in a small saucepan, then bring to the boil. Boil for 5 minutes or until the shallot has softened and the liquid is reduced and syrupy. Set aside.

4 Place the spring onions on the prepared tray. Make 3 insertions in the skin of the fish at the thicker end. Lay the fish on top of the spring onions, then drizzle with olive oil and rub with lemon juice and salt. Push some of the ginger slices into the incisions and place the remainder inside the cavity, along with the kaffir lime leaves. Bake the fish for 12 minutes, then flip over and continue to bake for a further 5 minutes or until just cooked through. Set aside to rest while you cook the potato scallops.

5 To cook the potato scallops, heat enough olive oil for deep-frying in a heavy-based frying pan over high heat until it registers 190°C on a sugar/deep-fry thermometer (or a cube of bread turns golden in 10 seconds). Dip the potato slices in the batter, allowing any excess to run off, then carefully place in the pan and fry for 1 minute on each side or until golden brown. Remove from the pan and drain on paper towel. Season with salt.

6 Serve the fish with the baked spring onions, potato scallops and lemon wedges alongside. Gently reheat the sauce and spoon over the fish or offer separately.

Strawberries
in vvio cotto with
crushed brown-sugar
meringues

STRAWBERRIES IN VINO COTTO
WITH CRUSHED BROWN-SUGAR MERINGUES

Serves 6

How often have you bought strawberries that looked wonderful – large and brightly coloured – yet upon biting into them you find that they aren't ripe? More often than not, I'd suggest. Although I've written for more years than I care to remember about never refrigerating strawberries as it dulls any flavour they may have, this applies to strawberries bought directly from a grower who has just picked them. Most strawberries you buy in shops will have been refrigerated, so unless you use them on the day you bought them, you'll need to keep them refrigerated too or they will become mouldy. In this case, I suggest it is best to keep them in the fridge, then take them out an hour or so before using them to bring to room temperature before cutting and drizzling them with a little vino cotto, as I've done here. It's truly magical how this simple step brings out their flavour so they actually taste as if they were picked ripe. The rest of this dessert is so simple it's child's play – however, not only children will love this!

500 g strawberries, hulled and cut in half
2 teaspoons vino cotto
500 g strawberry ice cream, such as Maggie
    Beer Strawberries and Cream Ice Cream
250 g creme fraiche

BROWN-SUGAR MERINGUES
¼ cup (55 g) firmly packed brown sugar
⅔ cup (150 g) caster sugar
4 free-range eggs, at room temperature,
    separated (from 59 g eggs)
salt
1 teaspoon verjuice
1 tablespoon cornflour

1 Preheat the oven to 120°C fan-forced (140°C conventional). Grease and line 2 baking trays with baking paper and set aside.

2 To make the meringues, place the brown sugar and caster sugar in a small mixing bowl and combine well, making sure there are no lumps. In the clean and dry bowl of an electric mixer, whisk the egg whites with a pinch of salt until very soft peaks form. With the motor running, slowly add the sugar mixture, a little at a time, whisking until the meringue is stiff and glossy. Fold in the verjuice and cornflour, then divide the mixture evenly into 15 meringues, spooning them onto the prepared baking trays as you go.

3 Bake the meringues for 45 minutes or until golden and dry. Turn off the oven and leave the meringues inside to cool completely with the door ajar (use a wooden spoon to wedge the door open).

4 Remove the meringues from the oven and roughly crush. Toss the strawberries in vino cotto and leave for 10 minutes.

5 Divide half of the crushed meringue among 6 plates, then top each with 2 generous scoops of ice cream. Spoon over the strawberries and a good tablespoon of creme fraiche, then finish off with more crushed meringue scattered over the top. Serve at once.

Acknowledgements

How do you begin to thank all the people involved in such an undertaking as this, or any book?

Perhaps firstly thanks should go to Julie Gibbs, my great friend and publisher extraordinaire, who is always that one step in front of the crowd. Making a book such as this is an intense creative process and Julie lured me with the promise that, not only would it be quick and simple to do, but that it would give me the chance to work with the renowned photographer Earl Carter – this got me over the line and, given it had to be shot pre- and post-Christmas, made the most frenetic shooting schedule I've ever encountered all worthwhile. So thank you, Jewels, for the chance to work with Earl. And thank you, Earl, particularly for that wonderful photograph of my messy sink – it encapsulates all the craziness of the shoot that I loved so much! Thanks also to stylists Matt Page and Vanessa Austin.

Huge thanks to Chris Wotton, whose irrepressible enthusiasm, energy and support make every day easier for me as we work together on product development; Dianne Wooldridge, who never shirks from a difficult task no matter how many hours in a day it might take (I even stole her from the Farmshop team for one of the shoots); and Cathy Radke, my assistant, who, as always, calmly tried to keep my life running amidst the chaos. And thanks must go to Damien Pignolet for allowing me to share his recipe for pate brisee in this book.

Thanks also to the team at Penguin: Julie's assistant, Josette Gardiner, who stepped in at the last moment on the first shoot and soothed any difficulties away; editor Kathleen Gandy, who had the difficult job of keeping me on task whilst always encouraging me; the uber-talented Art Director, Daniel New (and his team), whose design makes all the difference; Megan Pigott, who coordinated the logistics of the shoots so very well; and Production Controller Tracey Jarrett, who kept us on track with the deadlines – how lucky I am to have such a wonderful group to work with! And to Fiona Hammond – thanks again for testing my recipes with such care and attention.

Special thanks to my Colin, who, as ever, makes me laugh when I'm one step short of being hysterical, and copes with the house being turned upside-down. Thanks too to my daughters Saskia and Elli and grandchildren, Zöe, Max, Lilly, Rory and Ben, who actually hate to be photographed, but love to eat! And finally, to my friends in the choir, who allowed me to press them into these pages, showing what great fun we have singing together – thank you!

Index

A

Agresto 100–1
Aioli 330–1
almonds
  Cumquat, almond and chocolate
    tart 266–7
  Roasted almond jelly with cherry
    compote 158–9
Amaretto
  Espresso and Amaretto jellies 126
anchovies, *see* fish
apricots
  Apricot fool 233
  Dried apricot pavlova 228–9
artichokes
  Artichoke, pancetta and fior
    di latte pizza topping 316
  Lobster salad with waxy potatoes,
    preserved artichokes and tarragon
    mayonnaise 220–1
asparagus
  Red onion, asparagus and mozzarella
    pizza topping 317
aubergines, *see* eggplant
avocado
  Beer-battered mulloway with
    avocado, tomato and red onion
    salad 44
  Braised octopus with roasted
    smoked tomatoes, avocado and
    aioli 330–1
  Crab and avocado salad 23

B

Baba ghanoush 308–9
bacon and pancetta
  Artichoke, pancetta and fior di latte
    pizza topping 316
  Roast quail with figs and bacon
    and parmesan polenta 152–3
Baked chicken thighs with preserved
  lemon and rosemary 157
Baked flathead with ginger and
  vino cotto sauce and potato
  scallops 344–5
Baked peaches with ginger and lemon
  shortbread 260–1
Ballotine of Barossa chook 256–7
bananas
  Pavlova with lady finger banana
    and passionfruit topping 45
Barbecued corn on the cob 150
basil, *see* herbs

beef
  Slow-cooked fillet of beef 296–7
Beer family 5, 11, 163
Beer-battered mulloway with avocado,
  tomato and red onion salad 44
berries
  Peach and berry jelly trifle 236–7
  Raspberries in sparkling Shiraz
    jelly 121
  Strawberries in vino cotto
    with crushed brown-sugar
    meringues 348–9
biscuits
  Ginger and lemon shortbread 260–1
blue cheese
  Walnut bread with ripe blue cheese
    and honeycomb 272–3
Blue swimmer crab omelette 18
Bocconcini balls with dukkah 59
Braised octopus with roasted
  smoked tomatoes, avocado
  and aioli 330–1
brandy
  Christmas pudding with cumquat
    brandy butter 202–3
  Eggnog 136
breads and toasts
  Blue swimmer crab sandwiches
    with mustard bread and tomato
    and saffron jam 30
  Chicken schnitters 73
  Melba toast with my duck and
    orange pate 248
  Mustard bread rolls 32
  Olive-oil, olive and orange
    brioche 70–1
  Soft-boiled eggs on toast with caper,
    raisin and basil salsa 67
  Toasties two ways: ham and
    gruyere and goose and sour
    cherry jam 213
  Turkey salad with figs, bread and
    walnuts 216
  Walnut bread with ripe blue cheese
    and honeycomb 272–3
  Walnut flatbread 310
  Warm brioche and ice-cream
    sandwiches 224–5
brioches, *see* breads and toasts
Brown-sugar meringues 348–9
buffalo haloumi
  Eggplant with buffalo haloumi 141
  Haloumi with baba ghanoush and
    pomegranate dressing 308–9

burrata
  Figs with burrata and mint 174
butter
  Buttercream 124–5
  Buttered walnuts with rosemary 140
  Christmas pudding with cumquat
    brandy butter 202–3
  Pan-fried squid in butter and
    tarragon 341

C

capers
  Soft-boiled eggs on toast with caper,
    raisin and basil salsa 67
  Whiting sashimi with capers, chervil
    and lime 34
Caponata 146
capsicum (peppers)
  Roasted capsicum with Persian
    feta and eggplant and parsley
    salad 192–3
cheeses, *see* blue cheese; bocconcini;
  burrata; fior di latte; goat's curd;
  gruyere; haloumi; mozzarella;
  parmesan; Persian feta
cherries
  Goose and sour cherry jam
    toasties 213
  Ham, cherry and parsley verjuice
    jellies 219
  Roasted almond jelly with cherry
    compote 158–9
chervil, *see* herbs
Chestnut and chocolate pots with
  pineapple 81
chicken
  Baked chicken thighs with preserved
    lemon and rosemary 157
  Ballotine of Barossa chook 256–7
  Chicken, prune and lemon tarts with
    pine-nut mayonnaise 74–5
  Chicken schnitters 73
  Lemon-glazed chicken wings 80
chocolate
  Chestnut and chocolate pots with
    pineapple 81
  Chocolate ganache 81, 266–7
  Chocolate icing 124–5
  Cumquat, almond and chocolate
    tart 266–7
choir, meals with 2, 89
Christmas pudding with cumquat
  brandy butter 202–3

citrus, *see* cumquats; lemons;
  limes; oranges
Clotted cream 198–9
coffee
  Espresso and Amaretto jellies 126
corn
  Barbecued corn on the cob 150
crab
  Blue swimmer crab omelette 18
  Blue swimmer crab sandwiches with
    mustard bread and tomato and
    saffron jam 30
  Crab and avocado salad 23
  Crab cakes 22
  Crab-mustard mayonnaise 33
  Pasta with crab and roasted smoked
    tomatoes 29
  White gazpacho with blue swimmer
    crab 14–15
cream
  Apricot fool 233
  Buttercream (mock cream) 124–5
  Clotted cream 198–9
  Dill-cured ocean trout with
    horseradish cream 145
cucumber
  Cucumber and verjuice jelly with
    oysters 58
  Fattoush 149
Cumberland sauce 184–6
cumquats
  Christmas pudding with cumquat
    brandy butter 202–3
  Cumquat, almond and chocolate
    tart 266–7
  Cumquat and pistachio stuffing 256–7
  Cumquat stuffing 180–1
currants, *see* dried and glace fruits

D

desserts and sweet treats
  Apricot fool 233
  Baked peaches with ginger and
    lemon shortbread 260–1
  Chestnut and chocolate pots
    with pineapple 81
  Christmas pudding with cumquat
    brandy butter 202–3
  Cumquat, almond and chocolate
    tart 266–7
  Dried apricot pavlova 228–9
  Espresso and Amaretto jellies 126
  Nectarine tarte tatin 299
  Neenish tarts 124–5
  Pavlova with lady finger banana and
    passionfruit topping 45
  Peach and berry jelly trifle 236–7
  Poached white peaches with sparkling
    ruby jelly and clotted cream 198–9
  Raspberries in sparkling Shiraz
    jelly 121
  Roasted almond jelly with cherry
    compote 158–9
  Strawberries in vino cotto
    with crushed brown-sugar

  meringues 348–9
  Walnut bread with ripe blue cheese
    and honeycomb 272–3
  Warm brioche and ice-cream
    sandwiches 224–5
  see also puddings
Dill-cured ocean trout with
  horseradish cream 145
dressings
  Currant vinaigrette 40
  Pomegranate dressing 308–9
  Sumac dressing 149
  Verjuice vinaigrette 172
  Vinaigrette 216, 296–7
  Vino cotto vinaigrette 253
  see also mayonnaise; sauces
dried and glace fruits
  Chicken, prune and lemon tarts with
    pine-nut mayonnaise 74–5
  Cumquat, almond and chocolate
    tart 266–7
  Dried apricot pavlova 228–9
  Roast turkey with prune and
    orange stuffing and Cumberland
    sauce 184–6
  Sashimi of kingfish with umeboshi 284
  Soft-boiled eggs on toast with caper,
    raisin and basil salsa 67
  Tommy ruffs with currant
    vinaigrette 40
  Tuna rolls with currant and
    pine nut filling 334–5
drinks
  Eggnog 136
duck
  Melba toast with my duck and
    orange pate 248

E

eggplants (aubergines)
  Caponata 146
  Eggplant salad 96
  Eggplant with buffalo haloumi 141
  Haloumi with baba ghanoush and
    pomegranate dressing 308–9
  Roasted capsicum with Persian
    feta and eggplant and parsley
    salad 192–3
eggs
  Blue swimmer crab omelette 18
  Dried apricot pavlova 228–9
  Eggnog 136
  Pavlova with lady finger banana
    and passionfruit topping 45
  Sabayon 236–7
  Soft-boiled eggs on toast with caper,
    raisin and basil salsa 67
  Strawberries in vino cotto
    with crushed brown-sugar
    meringues 348–9
  Espresso and Amaretto jellies 126

F

Fattoush 149

fennel
  Garfish with fennel and orange
    salad 39
  Tea-smoked ocean trout with
    fennel 106–7
  Vino cotto-glazed quail with roasted
    smoked tomatoes and garlic and
    fennel salad 326–7
feta, *see* Persian feta
figs
  Figs with burrata and mint 174
  Pastry slabs with agresto, figs and
    prosciutto 100–1
  Pickled fig-glazed leg of ham 112–13
  Roast quail with figs and bacon and
    parmesan polenta 152–3
  Turkey salad with figs, bread
    and walnuts 216
fior di latte
  Artichoke, pancetta and fior
    di latte pizza topping 316
fish
  Baked flathead with ginger and
    vino cotto sauce and potato
    scallops 344–5
  Beer-battered mulloway with avocado,
    tomato and red onion salad 44
  Dill-cured ocean trout with
    horseradish cream 145
  Garfish with fennel and orange
    salad 39
  Sashimi of kingfish with umeboshi 284
  Squid with anchovy and Persian
    feta stuffing 337
  Tea-smoked ocean trout with
    fennel 106–7
  Tommy ruffs with currant
    vinaigrette 40
  Tuna rolls with currant and pine nut
    filling 334–5
  Whiting sashimi with capers,
    chervil and lime 34
flathead, *see* fish
fruits, *see names of specific fruits*

G

Garfish with fennel and orange salad 39
garlic
  Vino cotto-glazed quail with roasted
    smoked tomatoes and garlic and
    fennel salad 326–7
Gazpacho with sashimi prawn 250
gelatine, *see* jellies
ginger
  Baked flathead with ginger and
    vino cotto sauce and potato
    scallops 344–5
  Ginger and lemon shortbread 260–1
glace fruits, *see* dried and glace fruits
goat's curd
  Roasted vegetable and goat's curd
    pizza topping 320
goose
  Goose and sour cherry jam
    toasties 213

Roast goose with marmalade and
    cumquat stuffing and goose-fat
    roasted potatoes 180–1
grapes
    Roast pork loin with verjuice
        and grapes 190
    Salad of bitter leaves and grapes 253
gruyere
    Ham and gruyere toasties 213

H

haloumi
    Eggplant with buffalo haloumi 141
    Haloumi with baba ghanoush and
        pomegranate dressing 308–9
ham and prosciutto
    Ham, cherry and parsley verjuice
        jellies 219
    Ham and gruyere toasties 213
    Pan-fried green tomatoes and
        ham 212
    Pastry slabs with agresto, figs
        and prosciutto 100–1
    Pickled fig-glazed leg of ham 112–13
herbs
    Agresto 100–1
    Baked chicken thighs with preserved
        lemon and rosemary 157
    Buttered walnuts with rosemary 140
    Fattoush 149
    Figs with burrata and mint 174
    Pan-fried squid in butter and
        tarragon 341
    Soft-boiled eggs on toast with
        caper, raisin and basil salsa 67
    Tarragon mayonnaise 220–1
    Whiting sashimi with capers,
        chervil and lime 34
    see also parsley
Heritage tomato salad 288
honeycomb
    Walnut bread with ripe blue cheese
        and honeycomb 272–3
Horseradish cream 145

I

ice cream
    Warm brioche and ice-cream
        sandwiches 224–5
Icing 124–5

J

jams
    Goose and sour cherry jam
        toasties 213
    Tomato and saffron jam 33
jellies
    Cucumber and verjuice jelly
        with oysters 58
    Espresso and Amaretto jellies 126
    Ham, cherry and parsley verjuice
        jellies 219
    Peach and berry jelly trifle 236–7

Poached white peaches with sparkling
    ruby jelly and clotted cream 198–9
Raspberries in sparkling Shiraz
    jelly 121
Roasted almond jelly with cherry
    compote 158–9

K

kingfish, *see* fish

L

Lamb kibbeh 76
lemons
    Baked chicken thighs with preserved
        lemon and rosemary 157
    Chicken, prune and lemon tarts with
        pine-nut mayonnaise 74–5
    Ginger and lemon shortbread 260–1
    Lemon icing 124–5
    Lemon-glazed chicken wings 80
limes
    Lobster sashimi with rockmelon
        and lime 177
    Whiting sashimi with capers,
        chervil and lime 34
liqueurs, *see* Amaretto
lobster
    Lobster salad with waxy potatoes,
        preserved artichokes and tarragon
        mayonnaise 220–1
    Lobster sashimi with rockmelon
        and lime 177

M

mains
    Baked chicken thighs with preserved
        lemon and rosemary 157
    Baked flathead with ginger and
        vino cotto sauce and potato
        scallops 344–5
    Ballotine of Barossa chook 256–7
    Beer-battered mulloway with avocado,
        tomato and red onion salad 44
    Braised octopus with roasted
        smoked tomatoes, avocado
        and aioli 330–1
    Garfish with fennel and orange
        salad 39
    Pan-fried squid in butter and
        tarragon 341
    Pasta with crab and roasted
        smoked tomatoes 29
    Pickled fig-glazed leg of ham 112–13
    Roast goose with marmalade and
        cumquat stuffing and goose-fat
        roasted potatoes 180–1
    Roast pork loin with verjuice and
        grapes 190
    Roast quail with figs and bacon and
        parmesan polenta 152–3
    Roast turkey with prune and orange
        stuffing and Cumberland
        sauce 184-6

Roasted capsicum with Persian
    feta and eggplant and parsley
    salad 192–3
Slow-cooked fillet of beef 296–7
Squid-ink pasta with poached
    prawns 340
Squid risotto with roasted truss
    tomatoes 116–17
Squid with anchovy and Persian feta
    stuffing 337
Tea-smoked ocean trout with
    fennel 106–7
Tommy ruffs with currant
    vinaigrette 40
Tuna rolls with currant and pine nut
    filling 334–5
Vino cotto-glazed quail with roasted
    smoked tomatoes and garlic and
    fennel salad 326–7
mangoes
    Salad of paw paw, mango and
        rocket 195
mayonnaise
    Aioli 330–1
    Crab-mustard mayonnaise 33
    Pine-nut mayonnaise 74–5
    Tarragon mayonnaise 220–1
meat, *see* beef; lamb; pork; poultry
Melba toast with my duck and
    orange pate 248
menus 55, 91, 133, 167, 245, 281
meringues, *see* eggs
mint, *see* herbs
mozzarella
    Red onion, asparagus and mozzarella
        pizza topping 317
mulloway, *see* fish
Mustard bread rolls 32

N

nectarines
    Nectarine tarte tatin 299
    Salad of yabbies and nectarines 172
Neenish tarts 124–5
nuts, *see* almonds; pine nuts;
    pistachios; walnuts

O

ocean trout, *see* fish
octopus
    Braised octopus with roasted smoked
        tomatoes, avocado and aioli 330–1
Olive-oil, olive and orange brioche 70–1
onions
    Beer-battered mulloway with
        avocado, tomato and red
        onion salad 44
    Red onion, asparagus and mozzarella
        pizza topping 317
oranges
    Garfish with fennel and orange
        salad 39
    Melba toast with my duck and
        orange pate 248

Olive-oil, olive and orange
brioche 70–1
Roast turkey with prune and
orange stuffing and Cumberland
sauce 184–6
oysters
Cucumber and verjuice jelly
with oysters 58

P

pancetta, *see* bacon and pancetta
Pan-fried green tomatoes and ham 212
Pan-fried squid in butter and
tarragon 341
parmesan
Parmesan polenta 152–3
parsley
Fattoush 149
Ham, cherry and parsley verjuice
jellies 219
Parsley salad 193
passionfruit
Pavlova with lady finger banana
and passionfruit topping 15
pasta
Pasta with crab and roasted
smoked tomatoes 29
Squid ink pasta with poached
prawns 340
pastry
Damien Pignolet's pate brisee
(shortcrust pastry) 124–5
Pastry slabs with agresto, figs
and prosciutto 100–1
Sour-cream pastry 100–1
see also tarts
pate
Melba toast with my duck and
orange pate 248
pavlovas, *see* eggs
paw paw
Salad of paw paw, mango
and rocket 195
peaches
Baked peaches with ginger and
lemon shortbread 260–1
Peach and berry jelly trifle 236–7
Poached white peaches with
sparkling ruby jelly and
clotted cream 198–9
peppers, *see* capsicum
Persian feta
Persian feta-stuffed zucchini
flowers 64
Roasted capsicum with Persian
feta and eggplant and parsley
salad 193
Squid with anchovy and Persian
feta stuffing 337
pesto, *see* Agresto
Pickled fig-glazed leg of ham 112–13
pine nuts
Agresto 100–1
Chicken, prune and lemon tarts
with pine-nut mayonnaise 74–5

Tuna rolls with currant and
pine nut filling 334–5
pineapple
Chestnut and chocolate pots
with pineapple 81
pistachios
Cumquat and pistachio
stuffing 256–7
pizzas
Pizza topping 1: Artichoke, pancetta
and fior di latte 316
Pizza topping 2: Red onion,
asparagus and mozzarella 317
Pizza topping 3: Roasted vegetable
and goat's curd 320
Spelt pizza dough 321
Verjuice pizza dough 315–20
Poached white peaches with sparkling
ruby jelly and clotted cream 198–9
polenta
Roast quail with figs and bacon
and parmesan polenta 152–3
pomegranate molasses
Haloumi with baba ghanoush
and pomegranate dressing 308–9
pork
Roast pork loin with verjuice
and grapes 190
see also bacon and pancetta;
ham and prosciutto
Port Parham 1, 11
potatoes
Goose-fat roasted potatoes 180–1
Lobster salad with waxy potatoes,
preserved artichokes and tarragon
mayonnaise 220–1
Potato scallops 344–5
poultry, *see* chicken; duck; goose;
quail; turkey
prawns
Gazpacho with sashimi prawn 250
Squid-ink pasta with poached
prawns 340
preserved lemon, *see* lemons
prosciutto, *see* ham and prosciutto
prunes, *see* dried and glace fruits
puddings
Christmas pudding with cumquat
brandy butter 202–3

Q

quail
Roast quail with figs and bacon and
parmesan polenta 152–3
Vino cotto-glazed quail with roasted
smoked tomatoes and garlic and
fennel salad 326–7

R

radicchio
Salad of bitter leaves and grapes 253
raisins, *see* dried and glace fruits
Raspberries in sparkling Shiraz
jelly 121

red onions, *see* onions
red wine
Raspberries in sparkling Shiraz
jelly 121
risotto
Squid risotto with roasted truss
tomatoes 116–17
Roast goose with marmalade and
cumquat stuffing and goose-fat
roasted potatoes 180–1
Roast pork loin with verjuice and
grapes 190
Roast quail with figs and bacon
and parmesan polenta 152–3
Roast turkey with prune and
orange stuffing and Cumberland
sauce 184–6
Roasted almond jelly with cherry
compote 158–9
Roasted capsicum with Persian feta and
eggplant and parsley salad 193
Roasted vegetable salad 293
rocket
Salad of bitter leaves and grapes 253
Salad of paw paw, mango and
rocket 195
rockmelon
Lobster sashimi with rockmelon
and lime 177
rosemary, *see* herbs

S

Sabayon 236–7
saffron
Tomato and saffron jam 33
salads
Avocado, tomato and red
onion salad 44
Crab and avocado salad 23
Eggplant salad 96
Fattoush 149
Fennel and orange salad 39
Fennel salad 326–7
Heritage tomato salad 288
Lobster salad with waxy potatoes,
preserved artichokes and tarragon
mayonnaise 220–1
Parsley salad 193
Roasted vegetable salad 293
Salad of bitter leaves and grapes 253
Salad of paw paw, mango and
rocket 195
Salad of yabbies and nectarines 172
Turkey salad with figs, bread
and walnuts 216
salsas, *see* sauces
sandwiches, *see* breads and toasts
sashimi
Gazpacho with sashimi prawn 250
Lobster sashimi with rockmelon
and lime 177
Sashimi of kingfish with
umeboshi 284
Whiting sashimi with capers,
chervil and lime 34

sauces
  Agresto 100–1
  Caper, raisin and basil salsa 67
  Cumberland sauce 184–6
  Cumquat brandy butter 202–3
  Ginger and vino cotto sauce 344–5
  Horseradish cream 145
  see also dressings; jams; mayonnaise
seafood, *see* crab; lobster; octopus;
  prawns; squid; yabbies
Slow-cooked fillet of beef 296–7
Slow-cooked zucchini 101
Soft-boiled eggs on toast with caper,
  raisin and basil salsa 67
soups
  Gazpacho with sashimi prawn 250
  White gazpacho with blue
    swimmer crab 14–15
Sour-cream pastry 100–1
Sparkling ruby jelly 198–9
Spelt pizza dough 321
spirits, *see* brandy
squid
  Pan-fried squid in butter and
    tarragon 341
  Squid ink pasta with poached
    prawns 340
  Squid risotto with roasted truss
    tomatoes 116–17
  Squid with anchovy and Persian
    feta stuffing 337
Strawberries in vino cotto with crushed
  brown-sugar meringues 348–9
stuffings
  Anchovy and Persian feta
    stuffing 337
  Cumquat and pistachio
    stuffing 256–7
  Cumquat stuffing 180–1
  Prune and orange stuffing 184–6
Sumac dressing 149
sweet treats, *see* desserts and sweet treats

T

tarragon, *see* herbs
tarts
  Chicken, prune and lemon tarts with
    pine-nut mayonnaise 74–5
  Cumquat, almond and chocolate
    tart 266–7
  Nectarine tarte tatin 299
  Neenish tarts 124–5
  see also pastry
Tea-smoked ocean trout with
  fennel 106–7
Toasties two ways: ham and gruyere
  and goose and sour cherry jam 213
tomatoes
  Beer-battered mulloway with
    avocado, tomato and red
    onion salad 44
  Braised octopus with roasted
    smoked tomatoes, avocado
    and aioli 330–1

  Fattoush 149
  Heritage tomato salad 288
  Pan-fried green tomatoes and
    ham 212
  Pasta with crab and roasted
    smoked tomatoes 29
  Squid risotto with roasted truss
    tomatoes 116–17
  Tomato and saffron jam 33
  Vino cotto-glazed quail with roasted
    smoked tomatoes and garlic and
    fennel salad 326–7
Tommy ruffs with currant
  vinaigrette 40
trout, *see* fish
Tuna rolls with currant and
  pine nut filling 334–5
turkey
  Roast turkey with prune and
    orange stuffing and Cumberland
    sauce 184–6
  Turkey salad with figs, bread
    and walnuts 216

U

umeboshi
  Sashimi of kingfish with
    umeboshi 284

V

vegetables
  Roasted vegetable and goat's
    curd pizza topping 320
  Roasted vegetable salad 293
  see also names of specific vegetables
verjuice
  Agresto 100–1
  Cucumber and verjuice jelly
    with oysters 58
  Ham, cherry and parsley verjuice
    jellies 219
  Roast pork loin with verjuice
    and grapes 190
  Verjuice pizza dough 315
  Verjuice vinaigrette 172
vinaigrette, *see* dressings
vino cotto
  Baked flathead with ginger and
    vino cotto sauce and potato
    scallops 344–5
  Strawberries in vino cotto
    with crushed brown-sugar
    meringues 348–9
  Vino cotto vinaigrette 253
  Vino cotto-glazed quail with roasted
    smoked tomatoes and garlic and
    fennel salad 326–7

W

walnuts
  Buttered walnuts with rosemary 140
  Turkey salad with figs, bread
    and walnuts 216

  Walnut bread with ripe blue cheese
    and honeycomb 272–3
  Walnut flatbread 310
Warm brioche and ice-cream
  sandwiches 224–5
White gazpacho with blue
  swimmer crab 14–15
white peaches, *see* peaches
Whiting sashimi with capers,
  chervil and lime 34
wine, *see* red wine; vino cotto
witlof
  Salad of bitter leaves and grapes 253

Y

yabbies
  Salad of yabbies and nectarines 172

Z

zucchini and zucchini flowers
  Persian feta-stuffed zucchini
    flowers 64
  Slow-cooked zucchini 101

LANTERN

UK | USA | Canada | Ireland | Australia
India | New Zealand | South Africa | China

Penguin Books is part of the Penguin Random House group of companies whose
addresses can be found at global.penguinrandomhouse.com.

Penguin
Random House
Australia

First published by Penguin Group (Australia), 2013
This paperback edition published by Penguin Group (Australia), 2015

1 3 5 7 9 10 8 6 4 2

Design and illustrations by Daniel New © Penguin Group (Australia)
Design coordination by Hannah Schubert
Styling for food and incidental photography by Matt Page

Typeset in Livory and Alright Sans by Post Pre-Press Group
Colour separation by Splitting Image Colour Studio, Clayton, Victoria
Printed and bound in China by 1010 Printing International Limited

National Library of Australia
Cataloguing-in-Publication data:

Beer, Maggie, author.
Maggie's Christmas / Maggie Beer; photography by Earl Carter.
9781921384400 (pbk)
Christmas cooking--Australia.
Holiday cooking
Other Creators / Contributors: Carter, Earl, 1957- photographer.

641.568

penguin.com.au/lantern